Sacred Cow

Our Other Publications

Sri Chaitanya Chandramritam
Glories of Ekadasi
Sri Vrindaban Mahimamrta Complete Edition
Sri Srimad Bhagvata Arka Marichimala (New)
A Vasisnava Harmonium and Singing Method
Practical Mrdanga Lessons
Sri Krsna Leela Stava
Sri Radha Sahasra Nama
Sri Gopal Sahasra Nama
The Four Principle of Freedom
From Nothingness to Personhood
Heart of Devotion
Sri krsna Astottara-Sata Nama
Sri Krsna Caitanya Divya Sahasra Nama
Sri Gopala Tapani Upanisad
Sri Advaita Prakasa

If you are interested in the purchasing or the distribution of this book or any of the above publications. You may contact us.

ISBN 81-87812-56-7
Published By:
Rasbihari Lal & Sons.
Loi Bazar, Vrindaban-281121 (U.P.) India.
Phone: 91-565-2442570
Fax: 91-565-2443970
E-mail:
brijwasi2001@hotmail.com
Our Other Division
Brijwasi Exports

Sacred Cow

Translated by Bhūmipati dāsa
Edited by Pūrnaprajña dāsa

Dedicated to

His Divine Grace
A.C. Bhaktivedanta Swami Prabhupāda
founder-ācārya
International Society for Krishna Consciousness

Introduction

As a child, living in America, I heard that in India, cows are treated as sacred. I heard that even in the big cities of India, cows roamed freely, sometimes blocking traffic, and no one would disturb them. I thought that this was a good example of superstition. After all, for us, the cow was a food that I had been given by my mother since birth.

Many years later, I became convinced that eating meat is a terrible thing to do, and so I gave it up. Then, I came in contact with the International Society for Krishna Consciousness, in Boston. I received a small booklet containing three essays by His Divine Grace A. C. Bhaktivedanta Swami Prabhupāda, and upon reading it, I was astonished. Here was a person who answered all of life's important questions;

"Who am I?" "Who is God?" And, "What is the purpose of human life?" Thus it came to be that I accepted Śrīla Prabhupāda as my spiritual master, and after doing so, I studied his books very carefully.

Śrīla Prabhupāda emphasized that the understanding we get from sense perception is very limited and imperfect. All of us have four defects- we commit mistakes, we are illusioned, we have a cheating propensity, and our senses are imperfect. On the other hand, the understanding we receive from the Vedic literatures is perfect and without these four defects. Therefore, Śrīla Prabhupāda always recommended that we accept the Vedic understanding, even if it appears to contradict our common sense. Here is an example that Śrīla Prabhupāda often gave, and it is also mentioned in a verse of *Śrī Chaitanya Charitamrita:* Chaitanya Mahāprabhu said, "Conch shells and cow dung are nothing but the bones and the stool of some living entities, but according to the *Vedic* version they are both considered very pure."

In his purport, Śrīla Prabhupāda explains, "According to Vedic principles, bones and dung are generally considered very impure. If one touches a bone or stool, he must take a bath immediately. That is the Vedic injunction. Yet the Vedas also enjoin that a conch shell, although the bone of an animal and cow dung, although the stool of an animal, are very much sanctified. Even though such statements appear contradictory, on the basis of the Vedic version we still accept the fact that conch shells and cow dung are pure and sanctified."

The following is a conversation that took place in Moscow, when Śrīla Prabhupāda visited Professor Kotovsky:

Śrīla Prabhupāda: "As far as Vedic statements are concerned, they are infallible, and the scholars of the Vedas accept them in that way. For example, cow dung is the stool of an animal. Now, the Vedic statement is that as soon as you touch the stool of any animal—even if you touch your own stool—you are impure and have to purify yourself by taking a bath. According to the Hindu system, after evacuating one has to take a bath."

Prof. Kotovsky: "That is quite understandable hygienic knowledge."

Śrīla Prabhupāda: "But in another place it is stated that cow dung, although the stool of an animal, is pure. Even if you apply it to an impure place, that place becomes purified. This is superficially contradictory. In one place it is said that the stool of an animal is impure and as soon as you touch it you have to be purified, and in another place it says that cow dung is pure. According to our knowledge, it is contradictory—but still it is accepted by those who are followers of the Vedas. And the fact is that if you analyze cow dung, you will find that it contains all antiseptic properties."

Prof. Kotovsky: "This I don't know."

Śrīla Prabhupāda: "Yes, one professor in a medical college analyzed it, and he found it full of antiseptic properties. So Vedic statements, even if found contradictory, if analyzed scrutinizingly will prove correct. There may be an exception. But it is accepted, and when scientifically analyzed and examined, it is found to be correct."

Prof. Kotovsky: "Yes, if you analyze from the scientific point of view that is right."

Śrīla Prabhupāda: "There are other instances—for example, the conch shell. The conch shell is the bone of an animal and according to Vedic instruction if you touch the bone of an animal you become impure and have to take a bath. But this conch shell is kept in the Deity room, because it is accepted as pure by the Vedas. My point is that we accept Vedic laws without argument. That is the principle followed by scholars. If you can substantiate your statements by quotations from the Vedas, then they are accepted."

Elsewhere, Śrīla Prabhupāda explained, "Cow dung is accepted as purified and antiseptic. A person can keep stacks of cow dung in one place, and it will not create a bad odor to disturb anyone."

The other point about cows that Śrīla Prabhupāda emphasized again and again is that cows are considered one of the seven mothers. In a Bhagavad-gita lecture delivered in London in 1973, Śrīla Prabhupāda explained, "In India, in the villages, there is still the system amongst poor men, the cultivators, that if the cultivator cannot provide to keep a cow, he will not marry. So one should keep a wife only if he is able to keep a cow also. Because if you keep a wife, immediately there will be children. But if you cannot give them cows' milk, the children will be rickety, not very healthy. They must drink sufficient milk. So cow is therefore considered as mother."

"Because one mother has given birth to the child and another mother is supplying milk. So everyone should be obliged to mother cow, because she is supplying us milk. So according to our *shastra* there are seven mothers. The real mother from whose body I have taken my birth. Then there is the wife of my teacher. She is also mother. The wife of a *brahmana*, she is also a mother. Then, the queen is also a mother. Then *dhenu*. *Dhenu* means cow. She is also mother. And *dhatri*. Dhatri means nurse. Also the earth. Earth is also a mother. The people are taking care of mother land, where he is born. That is good. But they should take care of mother cow also. But they are not taking care of this mother. Therefore they are sinful. They must suffer. There must be war, pestilence, famine. As soon as people become sinful, immediately nature's punishment will come automatically. You cannot avoid it."

Śrī Chaitanya Mahāprabhu's discussion with Chand Kazi, as narrated in *Śrī Chaitanya Charitamrita*, is instructive in this regard:

The Lord said, "My dear uncle, I have come to your home just to ask you some questions."

"Yes," the Kazi replied, "You are welcome. Just tell me what is in Your mind."

The Lord said, "You drink cows' milk; therefore the cow is your mother. And the bull produces grains for your maintenance; therefore he is your father. Since the bull and cow are your father and mother, how can you kill and eat them? What kind of religious principle is this? On what strength are you so daring that you commit such sinful activities?"

In his purport to this verse, Śrīla Prabhupāda explains: "Everyone can understand that we drink the milk of cows and take the help of bulls in producing agricultural products. Therefore, since our real father gives us food grains and our mother gives us milk with which to live, the cow and bull are considered our father and mother."

"According to Vedic civilization, there are seven mothers, of which the cow is one. Therefore Śrī Chaitanya Mahāprabhu challenged the Muslim Kazi, 'What kind of religious principle do you follow by killing your father and mother to eat them?' In any civilized human society, no one would dare kill his father and mother for the purpose of eating them. Therefore Śrī Chaitanya Mahāprabhu challenged the system of Muslim religion as patricide and matricide. In the Christian religion also, a principal commandment is 'Thou shalt not kill.' Nevertheless, Christians violate this rule; they are very expert in killing and in opening slaughterhouses."

"In our Krishna consciousness movement, our first provision is that no one should be allowed to eat any kind of flesh. It does not matter whether it is cows' flesh or goats' flesh, but we especially stress the prohibition against cows' flesh because according to *shastra* the cow is our mother."

Another thing to carefully consider is that when Lord Krishna, the Supreme Personality of Godhead, appeared on this Earth, He acted as a cowherd boy. His entire day was devoted to taking care of the cows and the calves. If the Supreme Lord takes such care of the cows, they why shouldn't we? This small book contains a selection of verses from *shastra* giving us a good idea of the importance of cows. I am confident that anyone who reads it will gain a better appreciation of their importance.

The editor

Sacred Cow

It is sometimes said, "There is more to it than meets the eye." This means that ordinary sense perception is limited, and so cannot disclose the whole truth of a matter. For example, we understand from *Bhagavad-gītā* that the material body is but a covering, a dress of the soul. And yet, with our eyes, we can only see the external body- we cannot see the eternal soul. It is for this reason that Shrila Prabhupada repeatedly urged us to consider *shastra chaksu* (the eye of *shastra*) to be more important than our material eyes.

We may look at a cow and think that it is just an ordinary animal, like all others, such as dogs, cats and donkeys. But, if we see through the eyes of *shastra*, we will understand a truth that is far beyond the perception of our senses. This book is presented for that purpose. It will allow us to understand the truth about cows, beyond any ordinary, materialistic conception.

Śrīla Vyāsadeva divided the *Vedas*, and also compiled many scriptures like *Mahābhārata*, the *Purāṇas*, *Vedānta sutras* and *Yoga darśana*. The entire range of Vedic literatures is his unique contribution. In all of his literature, he gave a special place to the cow. Major portions of the *Purāṇas* deal with the glories of the cow. The religious principle, or dharma, has been compared with Vṛṣabha, the bull. He wrote in the *Purāṇas* that the *Vedas* and sacrifice are the two best means for the protection of this world, and that both of these are supported by cow products like milk and ghee. Actually, the brāhmaṇas, the *Vedas*, and the cows are one and the same.

The cow is extremely pure. Therefore, wherever she is present, that place cannot be polluted. The cow is considered to be the gateway to heaven. She is all-auspicious, and the supplier of food to both the demigods and human beings. Vedavyāsa also described that the Supersoul lives within the body, just like milk. He cannot be seen from outside, but can be perceived through the study of the scriptures.

In the *Mahābhārata*, there is an entire chapter dedicated to the worship of the cow. His father, the sage Parāśara, wrote a book called *Kṛṣi parāśara*, in which he glorified the cow and the bull. Cows should be treated politely. They should be kept in a cowshed. When sick, they should be treated properly. The cowshed should be free from all types of fear. There should be arrangements to keep the cows aloof from excessive cold, heat and rain. There should be pasturing grounds for the cows in every village.

Lord Kṛṣṇa used to always protect the cows whenever they faced any danger. He was always concerned about the cows and the Brajavāsīs' happiness. Kṛṣṇa killed Aghāśura and delivered the cowherd boys and the calves from the mouth of that demon. He chastised Kāliya and made the water of the Yamunā, as well as the pasturing ground, free from poison. He drank forest fires two times, and saved all the inhabitants of Braja, including the cows. His pastimes are all explained in the *Śrīmad-Bhāgavatam* .

Not only did He protect the inhabitants of Braja, He also demonstrated that service to the cows is the main profession of Vaiṣyas, and particularly the Brajavāsīs. This is stated in *Śrīmad-Bhāgavatam* , 10/24/21:

kṛṣi-vāṇijya-go-rakṣā
kusīdaṁ tūryam ucyate
vārtā catur-vidhā tatra
vayaṁ go-vṛttayo 'niśam

"The occupational duties of the vaiśya are conceived in four divisions: farming, commerce, cow protection and moneylending. Out of these, we as a community are always engaged in cow protection."

Based on this principle, Kṛṣṇa stopped the sacrifice for pleasing Indra and introduced the worship of Govardhan Hill. This made Indra angry and so he tried to inundate the whole of Braja with water. Indeed, Indra caused an incessant rainstorm in Braja, but Kṛṣṇa by His supreme prowess effortlessly lifted Govardhan Hill in His left hand and protected all the inhabitants, including the cows and calves. This is described in *Śrīmad-Bhāgavatam* 10/24/20:

Whenever Kṛṣṇa used to play His flute, the cows and calves would come running to Him. In the *Śrīmad-Bhāgavatam* 10/14/12 it is stated:

megha-gambhīrayā vācā
nāmabhir dūra-gān paśūn
kvacid āhvayati prītyā
go-gopāla-manojñayā

dhenavo manda-gāminya
ūdho-bhāreṇa bhūyasā
yayur bhagavatāhūtā
drutaṁ prītyā snuta-stanāḥ

"When the cows and calves would go to a far away forest and Kṛṣṇa would affectionately yet gravely call them by their names, they would become completely overwhelmed by love for Kṛṣṇa. Milk would begin to fall from their milk bags and they would come running to Kṛṣṇa. In *Śrīmad-Bhāgavatam* (10/21/13), the following verse is also found in regard to the cows' love for Kṛṣṇa:

gāvaś ca kṛṣṇa-mukha-nirgata-veṇu-gīta
pīyūṣam uttabhita-karṇa-puṭaiḥ pibantyaḥ
śāvāḥ snuta-stana-payaḥ-kavalāḥ sma tasthur
govindam ātmani dṛśāśru-kalāḥ spṛśantyaḥ

"When Kṛṣṇa used to play His flute, the cows of Braja would become completely enchanted by the sweet sound. Their ears would stand erect, as if they were drinking nectar. It appeared that they embraced Kṛṣṇa within their hearts. Tears of love would flow from their eyes. The condition of the calves would appear even more pathetic. They would be so stunned that they could neither drink milk nor stop drinking. They used to feel Kṛṣṇa's warm touch in their hearts."

Upon seeing Kṛṣṇa's enchanting beauty, the cows, the birds, deer and other creatures would become overwhelmed with ecstatic love so that the hair on their bodies would stand on end.

Not only the cows felt such ecstasy. Even Govardhan Hill became the topmost devotee and worshipable because it was engaged in the service of the cows and the Supreme Lord. In the *Śrīmad-Bhāgavatam* , 10/21/18, it is stated:

> *hantāyam adrir abalā hari-dāsa-varyo*
> *yad rāma-kṛṣṇa-caraṇa-sparaśa-pramodaḥ*
> *mānaṁ tanoti saha-go-gaṇayos tayor yat*
> *pānīya-sūyavasa-kandara-kandamūlaiḥ*

"Girirāja Govardhan is glorious because it supplies for Kṛṣṇa and Balarāma many caves for Their rest, fruits and roots for Their food, water and green grass for the cows."

Lord Kṛṣṇa considered the cow as non-different from His form and as such, the cows and gopīs became the center point of all His pastimes in Braja. Kṛṣṇa was their protector, servant, friend, and their everything. There was no festival in Braja that was performed without the presence of cows and cow products. From His very birth, Lord Kṛṣṇa, along with Balarāma, Their parents, and all the inhabitants of Braja lived in the association of cows. On the occasion of Kṛṣṇa's birth, Nanda Mahārāja gave away innumerable cows in charity. In *Śrīmad-Bhāgavatam* , 10/5/7 it is stated:

gāvo vṛṣā vatsatarā
haridrā-taila-rūṣitāḥ
vicitra-dhātu-barhasrag-
vastra-kāñcana-mālinaḥ

"The cows, bulls and calves were thoroughly smeared with a mixture of turmeric and oil, mixed with varieties of minerals. Their heads were bedecked with peacock feathers, and they were garlanded and covered with cloth and golden ornaments."

After the killing of Pūtana, the gopīs, in order to protect Kṛṣṇa from further inauspiciousness, touched the tail of a cow to His head, bathed Him with cow urine and smeared cow dung all over His body. This is stated in *Śrīmad-Bhāgavatam* , 10/6/19 & 20

yaśodā-rohiṇībhyāṁ tāḥ
samaṁ bālasya sarvataḥ
rakṣāṁ vidadhire samyag
go-puccha-bhramaṇādibhiḥ

go-mūtreṇa snāpayitvā
punar go-rajasārbhakam
rakṣāṁ cakruś ca śakṛtā
dvādaśāṅgeṣu nāmabhiḥ

"Thereafter, mother Yaśodā and Rohiṇī, along with the other elderly gopīs, waved about the switch of a cow to give full protection to the child Śrī Kṛṣṇa."

"The child was thoroughly washed with cow urine and then smeared with the dust raised by the movements of the cows. Then different names of the Lord were applied with cow dung on twelve different parts of His body, beginning with the forehead, as done in applying tilaka. In this way, the child was given protection."

When Kṛṣṇa was kidnapped by the demon, Tṛṇāvarṭa, mother Yaśodā became so aggrieved that she was compared to a cow who had lost her calf. (*Śrīmad-Bhāgavatam* 10/7/24).

When Kṛṣṇa and Balarāma's name giving ceremony was performed, Gargamuni chose the cowshed as the venue.

Lord Kṛṣṇa took the forms of calves and cowherd boys and drank milk from their respective mothers. In this way, the Lord made their lives successful. Brahmā became astonished to see these pastimes of the Lord. He prayed, (*Śrīmad-Bhāgavatam* 10/14/31)

aho 'ti-dhanyā vraja-go-ramaṇyaḥ
stanyāmṛtaṁ pītam atīva te mudā
yāsāṁ vibho vatsatarātmajātmanā
yat-tṛptaye 'dyāpi na cālam adhvarāḥ

"O almighty Lord, how greatly fortunate are the cows and ladies of Vṛndāvana, the nectar of whose breast milk You have happily drunk to Your full satisfaction, taking the form of their calves and children! All the Vedic sacrifices performed from time immemorial up to the present day have not given You as much satisfaction."

The Ideal Example of Serving the Cow was Given by Kṛṣṇa and Balarāma.

This is stated in *Śrīmad-Bhāgavatam* 10/11/45 as follows:

tau vatsa-pālakau bhūtvā
sarva-lokaika-pālakau
saprātar-āśau go-vatsāṁś
cārayantau viceratuḥ

"Kṛṣṇa and Balarāma, who are the maintainers of the universe, used to go to the field for tending the calves. They wandered about in the various forests barefoot. Although Nanda and Yaśodā requested Them many times to put on Their shoes, They refused because the calves were also barefoot. When Kṛṣṇa used to walk in the forest, the gopīs felt great distress because of separation from him."

In the *Śrīmad-Bhāgavatam* 10/31/11 it is stated:

calasi yad vrajāc cārayan paśūn
nalina-sundaraṁ nātha te padam
śila-tṛṇāṅkuraiḥ sīdatīti naḥ
kalilatāṁ manaḥ kānta gacchati

"My dear Lord, our hearts become overwhelmed with distress, thinking how much pain You must be feeling in Your feet because of walking barefoot in the forest while tending the cows. Your soft and beautiful lotus feet must be pained by particles of stone, thorns and harsh grass."

Kṛṣṇa enjoyed many pastimes with the cows and their calves. Sometimes He would kiss them and sometimes He would feed them soft, green dhurvā grass, and sometimes He would make them drink water from His own hands.

The cows, bulls and calves have so much love for Śrī Kṛṣṇa. This was displayed when Kṛṣṇa was captured by the serpent Kāliya. This is stated in the *Śrīmad-Bhāgavatam* 10/16/11.

gāvo vṛṣā vatsataryaḥ
krandamānāḥ su-duḥkhitāḥ
kṛṣṇe nyastekṣaṇā bhītā
rudantya iva tasthire

"The cows, the bulls, and the male and female calves became greatly afflicted in their hearts. They were stunned and began to cry. Not able to do anything, they simply looked at Kṛṣṇa helplessly."

The Ancient Medical Science Prescribed in the Vedas, called Ayurveda, stesses the importance of the cow in maintaining good health.

Ayurveda is very ancient scripture. It is part of *Atharva Veda*. It is eternal and beginningless. According to *Ayurveda*, the cow is our mother. She is the backbone of Vedic culture. Her position is very elevated and her glories have been widely spread since the time of creation. The cow is considered the residence of the demigods and the form of the universe. In ancient times, the sages and the spiritual masters used to keep cows in their *āśramas*. Their students were supposed to look after these cows. Because of the hard labor involved in the service of the cows, the students' health remained always fit. They were not attacked by any illnesses.

Cow Milk — There is no food in the whole world more nutritious than cow's milk. That is why another name of milk is nectar. When a baby is born, his main food for the first three years is milk. A baby who has no mother can survive on cow milk. Milk is never prohibited during any stage of life, beginning from birth up to the time of death. As far as health is concerned, milk is considered a complete food. Cow milk contains every nutrient that is required for the growth of the human body. It increases the physical, mental and spiritual power of human beings. In ancient times, the sages, as well as ordinary people, used to drink milk and lead healthy lives. In the Suśruta saṁhītā, milk is said to be the food for all living entities. In the Caraka-saṁhītā, milk is accepted as the sustainer of life.

Cow's milk is very useful for the human body. It slows down the process of ageing, and cures many diseases. It is especially useful for those who are weak and injured. It increases intelligence and strength, it removes fatigue, checks giddiness, regulates the breathing, reduces coughing, removes hunger- and cures fever, haematemesis and many other illnesses. It regulates and increases the duration of life.

Cow Yogurt— It is best for giving strength to the body. It makes food tasty, nourishing and pure. It helps stimulate the body and it removes gas. Cow yogurt is most effective among other yogurts. Buttermilk made from cow yogurt balances the three faults caused by mucus, bile and air. It is stimulating and tasty- it increases intelligence, and it cures piles and stomach ailments.

Cow Butter— It is very beneficial for the body. It makes one fair, strong, and bright. It purifies the air, bile and blood. It cures tuberculosis, piles and coughing. It is very essential, especially for children.

Cow Ghee— It makes one's complexion shining, it enhances one's memory, increases one's strength, nourishes the body, regulates any air and mucus imbalance, removes tiredness, destroys bile, cures heart disease, and increases the fire in the stomach. It is very tasty, it keeps the body fit, it is useful for sacrifice, it possesses many good qualities and it is attained due to good fortune.

Cow Urine and Cow Dung— They are warm, bitter and strong in taste. Because they contain sodium, they stop gas disorders. They cure all ailments born from mucus, bile and gas. Cow urine is useful in acidity, stomach disease and many other illnesses. According to *Ayurveda*, cow urine removes leprosy and other skin diseases. Cow dung is a purifying agent. It is smeared inside and outside the house, to keep it purified. It is also used as a pesticide. The cow and cow products are incomparable in the eyes of *Ayurveda*. By service to the cow, all perfection is achieved. Cow protection is very necessary for the preservation of *Ayurveda*.

Aside from awarding good health, the cow is beneficial in numerous ways.

The Cow is the Giver of Liberation and She is the Form of all Holy Places

In the *Śrī Kṛṣṇa-janma-khaṇḍa* section of *Brahma-vaivarta Purāṇa* 21/ 91 to 93 it is stated:

sarve devā gavām aṅge
tīrthāni tat-padeṣu ca

tad-guhyeṣu svayaṁ lakṣmīs
tiṣṭhaty eva sadā pitaḥ

goṣ-padākta-mṛdā yo hi
tilakaṁ kurute naraḥ
tīrtha-snāto bhavet sadyo
'bhayaṁ tasya pade pade

gāvas tiṣṭhanti yatraiva
tat tīrthaṁ parikīrtitam
prāṇāṁs tyaktvā naras tatra
sadyo mukto bhaved dhruvam

"All of the demigods live in the bodies of cows. The holy places live in the cow's legs. Lakṣmī lives in the cow's heart. A person who puts tilaka on his forehead with the mud that has touched a cow's hoof at once attains the result of bathing in a holy place. He attains victory at every step. A place where cows stay is considered sanctified, and a person who dies there certainly attains liberation."

Prayers to the Cow From Ṛg Veda

mātā rudrāṇāṁ duhitā vasūnāṁ
svasādityānām amṛtasya nābhiḥ
pra nu vocaṁ cikituṣe janāya
mā gāmanā gām aditiṁ vadhiṣṭa

"The cow is the mother of the Rudras, and the daughter of the Vasus. She is the sister of the Ādityas and a source of nectar in the form of Ghee. To all thoughtful men I advise: never kill an innocent cow."

ā gāvo agmannuta bhadramakran
sīdantu goṣṭhe raṇayantvasme
prajāvatīḥ pururūpā iha syurindrāya
pūrvīruṣaso duhānāḥ

"May the cow come to our house and benefit us. May she happily stay in our cowshed and surcharge the whole atmosphere with her beautiful sounds. May the cow give us her milk early in the morning, to be used for the worship of the almighty Supersoul."

na tā naśanti na dabhāti taskaro
nāsāmāmitro vyathirādadharṣati
devāṁśca yābhiryajate dadāti ca
jyogit tābhiḥ sacate gopatiḥ saha

"The cows are neither inauspicious, nor anyone can steal her, nor can an enemy give her trouble. By the help of a cow, a householder is able to worship the demigods and give charity to others. May she remain perpetually with them."

gāvo bhago gāva indro me achān gāvaḥ
somasya prathamasya bhakṣaḥ
imā yā gāvaḥ sa janāsa indra
ichāmīd dhṛdāmanasā cidindram

"May cows become our principle wealth. May Indra give us wealth in the form of cows, may cows' milk mixed with somarasa become the main ingredient for performing sacrifice. Those who possess cows are almost on a level with Indra. I wish to faithfully worship the Supreme Lord with the products of cows."

yūyaṁ gāvo medayathā kṛśaṁ
cidaśrīraṁ cit kṛṇuthā supratīkam
bhadraṁ gṛhaṁ kṛṇutha bhadravāco
bṛhad vo vaya ucyate sabhāsu

"O cows, you make unhealthy people healthy, and ugly people beautiful. By your auspicious sound, you also make our house auspicious. That is why your glories are sung in the assembly of righteous people."

prajāvatīḥ sūyavasaṁ riśantīḥ śuddhā
apaḥ suprapāṇepibantīḥ
mā va stena īśata māghaśaṁsaḥ
pari vo hetī rudrasya vṛjyāḥ

"O cows, may you have many calves. May you get sufficient food and may you drink pure water from a lake. May you never fall into the trap of miscreants, and may the weapon of Rudra always protect you."

Gavopaniṣada

Saudāsa uvāca

trailakye bhagavan kiṁsvit
pavitraṁ kathyate' nagha
yat kirtayan sadā martyaḥ
prāpnuyāt puṇyam uttamam

Saudāsa said, "O my lord! O sinless sage, what is that pure object within the three worlds that simply by taking its name, human beings can accumulate great piety?"

Vaśiṣṭha uvāca

gāvaḥ surabhi gandhinyas
tathā guggulu gandhayaḥ

gāvaḥ pratiṣṭhā bhūtānām
gāvaḥ svastyanaṁ mahat

The great sage Vaśiṣṭha said, "O King, many varieties of aroma emanate from the body of a cow. As such, many cows are as fragrant as *guggula* resin. The cow is the support of all living entities, and the ocean of auspiciousness."

gāvo bhūtaṁ ca bhavyaṁ ca
gāvaḥ puṣṭiḥ sanātanī
gāvo lakṣmās tathā mūlaṁ
goṣu dattaṁ na naśyati

"The cow is the past and future. She nourishes the health of all living entities, and she is the root of prosperity. The piety one achieves by feeding a cow is never destroyed."

annaṁ hy paramam gāvo
devānāṁ paramaṁ haviḥ
svāhakāra vaṣaṭ kārau
goṣu nityaṁ pratiṣṭhitau

"The cow is the cause of one's accumulation of food grains. She awards the best sacrificial ingredients to the demigods. The sacrifice of the demigods and the sacrifice of Indra are both performed on the basis of the cow."

gāvo yajñasya hy phalaṁ
goṣu yajñāḥ pratiṣṭhitaḥ
gāvo bhaviśyaṁ bhūtaṁ ca
goṣu yajñāḥ pratiṣṭhitaḥ

"It is the cow which awards the result of sacrifice. The performance of sacrifice is dependent upon her. She is the past and future. All sacrifices are based upon her."

sāyaṁ prātaśca satataṁ
homa kāle mahādyute
gāvo dadati vai homyam
ṛṣibhyaḥ puruṣarsabha

"O greatly powerful king, every morning and evening when the sages perform fire sacrifices, it is the cow who supplies them the essential ingredients, in the form of ghee, etc."

yāni kāni ca durgāṇi
duṣkṛtāni kṛtāni ca

taranti caiva papmānaṁ
dhenuṁ ye dadati prabho

"My dear King, those who give milk cows in charity become liberated from all types of danger, and also become free from all sinful reactions."

ekāṁ ca daśagurdadyāt
daśa dadyātcca gośati
śataṁ sahasra gurdadyāt
sarve tulya phaḷā hy te

"One who has ten cows should donate one cow, one who has one hundred cows should donate ten cows, and one who has one thousand cows should donate one hundred cows. All of these persons are eligible to achieve the same amount of piety."

anāhitāgniḥ satagur
yajvā ca sahasra guḥ
samṛddho yaśca kināśo
nārdhyamarhanti te trayaḥ

"A person who does not perform agnihotra sacrifices, even after keeping one hundred cows, a person who does not perform fire sacrifices, despite possessing one thousand cows, and a person who does not give up miserliness, are not fit to be shown any respect."

kapilāṁ ye prayacchanti
sa vatsāṁ kāṁsya dohanām
subratāṁ vastra saṁvītām
ubhau lokau jayanti te

"A person who donates a brown cow that is full of auspicious symptoms, along with her calf, and also donates a pot made of bell metal for milking the cow, conquers both this world and the next."

yuvānam indriyopetaṁ
śatena śata yuṭhapaṁ
gavendram brāhmaṇendrāya
bhūri śṛṅgaṁ alaṅkṛtam

vṛṣabhaṁ ye prayacchanti
śrotriyāya parantapa
aiśvaryaṁ te' dhigacchanti
jāya mānāḥ punaḥ punaḥ

"O destroyer of the enemy, those who donate one hundred healthy, strong, nicely decorated bulls, that have strong horns, along with one hundred cows, to a qualified brāhmaṇa who is expert in the knowledge of the *Vedas*, certainly achieve great wealth in this life and in future lives as well."

nā kīrtayitvā gāha supyāt
tāsāṁ saṁsmṛtya cotpatet
sāyāṁ prātar namasye ca
gāstataḥ puṣtimāpnuyāt

"Do not go to bed at night without praising cows. Do not get up in the morning without remembering the cow. Offer respect to the cow daily, in the morning. By doing so, a human being achieves strength and nourishment."

gavāṁ mūtra puriṣasya
nodvijeta kathañcana

na cāsāṁ māṁsa maśnīyād
gavāṁ puṣṭiṁ tathāpnuyāt

"Do not hate cow urine and cow dung. Never eat cow meat. By following this advice, human beings can become prosperous."

gāśca saṅkīrtaye nityaṁ
nāva manyeta tāstathā
aniṣṭaṁ svapramālakṣya
gāṁ naraḥ samprakīrtayet

"Chant the name of the cow daily and never insult her. If one sees a bad dream, one should immediately remember the cow."

gomayena sadā snāyāt
kariṣe cāpi saṁviśot

śleṣma mūtra purīṣāṇi
pratighātaṁ ca varjayet

"Before taking a daily bath, apply cow dung. Sit down on a place smeared with cow dung. Do not spit, urinate and pass stool upon cow dung. Always avoid hitting cows."

ghṛtena juhuyādagni
ghṛtena svasti vācayet
ghṛtaṁ dadyāt ghṛtaṁ prāśod
gavāṁ puṣṭiṁ sadāśnute

Use ghee in fire sacrifices. Use ghee in all auspicious activities. Donate ghee and also use it for personal necessities. By doing this, the human beings will always support the cows and understand their value.

gomatyā vidyayā dhenuṁ
tīlānāṁ abhimantrya yaḥ
sarva ratra mayiṁ daddyātra
sa śocet kṛtākṛte

A person who donates a cow to a qualified brahmana, along with sesame seed, after duly performing the necessary ritual, does not have to suffer the consequences of his pious and sinful activities.

gāvo maṁupatiṣṭhantu
hema śṛṅgyāḥ payo mucaḥ
surabhya saurabhe yaśca
saritaḥ sāgaraṁ yathā

As the rivers flow into the ocean, may Surabhi and Saurabheyi cows that give milk and have horns covered with gold, come to me.

gāvai paśyāṁyahaṁ nityaṁ
gāvaḥ paśyantu māṁ sadā
gāvo' smākaṁ vayaṁ tāsāṁ
yato gāvastato vayaṁ

May I always see the cow and may the cow always see me. The cow belongs to me and I belong to the cow. I wish to live in a place where cows live.

evaṁ rātrau divā cāpi
sameṣu viṣameṣu ca
mahābhayeśu ca naraḥ
kīrtayan mucchyate bhayāt

A person who, either during the day or at night, either in happiness or at a time of fearful conditions, remembers or glorifies the cow, certainly becomes freed from all fearful conditions.

Circumambulating the cow:

gavāṁ dṛṣṭvā namaskṛtya
kuryācciva pradakṣiṇaṁ
pradakṣiṇī kṛtā tena
saptadvipā vasundharā

mātaraḥ sarvabhūtānāṁ
gāvaḥ sarva sukha pradāḥ
vṛddhiṁ ākāṁśatā nityaṁ
gāvaḥ kāryāḥ pradakṣināḥ

One should see, offer obeisances to, and circumambulate the cow. By doing so, one is supposed to have circumambulated the entire earth, with it's seven islands. The cow is the mother of all. She gives happiness to everyone. People who desire prosperity should daily circumambulate the cow.

Gomati-vidyā

from *Viṣṇu-dharmottara* Part II – 42/49 to 58

gomatiṁ kītayiṣyāmi
sarva pāpa praṇāśinīṁ
tāṁ tu me vadato vipra
śṛṇusva susamāhitaḥ

gāvaḥ surabhayo nityaṁ
gāvo guggula gandhikāḥ
gāvaḥ pratiṣṭhā bhūtānāṁ
gāvaḥ svastyayanaṁ paraṁ

annameva paraṁ gāvo
devānāṁ haviruttamaṁ
pāvanaṁ sarvabhūtānāṁ
rakṣanti ca vahanti ca

haviṣā mantra pūtena
tarpayantya marāṇdivi
ṛṣināṁ agnihotreṣu
gāvo home prayojitāḥ

sarveṣām eva bhūtānāṁ
gāvaḥ saranaṁuttamam
gāvaḥ pavitraṁ paramaṁ
gāvo maṅgalaṁ uttamam

gāvaḥ svargasya sopānaṁ
gāvo dhanyāḥ sanātanaḥ
namo gobhyaḥ śrīmatibhyaḥ
saurabheyibhya eva ca

namo brahmasutābhyaśca
pavitrābhyo namo namaḥ
brāhmaṇāścaiva gāvaśca
kulaṁekaṁ dvidhā sthitaṁ

ekatra mantrās tiṣṭhanti
havir ekatra tiṣṭhati
deva brāhmaṇa gosādhu
sādhvibhiḥ sakalaṁ jagat

dharyate yai sadā taśmāt
sarve pujyatamāḥ sadā
yatra tīrthe sadā gāvaḥ
pibanti tṛṣitā jalaṁ

uttaranti pathā yena
sthitā tatra sarasvatī
gavāṁ hy tīrthe vasatīḥ
gangā puṣṭistathā
tadrajasi pravṛddhā
lakṣmīḥ kariṣe praṇatau ca
dharmastāsāṁ praṇāmam
satataṁ ca kuryāt

"In reply to the question of Puṣkara, the son of Varuṇa, Lord Paraśurāma described this *gomati-vidyā*: 'O great brāhmaṇa, now I will reveal to you the gomati-vidyā which uproots all sinful reactions. Hear this with full attention. The cow, who is another form of Surabhi, is the eternal mother of the universe. She is sacred, beautiful and as fragrant as *guggula*.' "

" 'The existence of all living entities depends upon the cow. She awards all of life's objectives. She is the main cause of the production of all types of food grains. She is also the cause of the ingredients and the food offered in sacrifice to the demigods. Simply by her touch and sight, she purifies all living entities. She produces nectarean objects like milk, yogurt and ghee. Her calves, when grown up as bulls, carry heavy loads and help produce food grains. By her milk products she helps the demigods perform sacrifices.' "

" 'All the great sages use cow products as ingredients for their various activities. The cow gives shelter to one who has no shelter. Among all purified objects, she is the most pure, and among all auspicious objects, she is the most auspicious.' "

" 'The cow is the support by which one can directly transfer himself to heaven. She is also the perpetual cause of one's wealth and prosperity. I offer my obeisances to the cow, in whose body Lakṣmī resides. I offer my respect to the beautiful cow, for she is pure, simple and aromatic. I bow down before the cow, who is the daughter of Brahmā. She is pure, internally and externally, and she keeps the whole atmosphere pure by her presence. I repeatedly offer my obeisances to her.' "

" 'Actually, the cow and the brāhmaṇa belong to the same family. Both are situated in the mode of goodness. If *brāhmaṇas* are qualified to recite Vedic mantras, then cows will supply ingredients for their sacrifices. Only by the combination of both, the brahmanas and the cows, is the performance of sacrifice for the pleasure of Viṣṇu complete. The cow is the support of the entire world, as well as all of the demigods, the brāhmaṇas, the saintly persons, the chaste ladies and other pious beings. She is always worshipable.' "

" 'Wherever the thirsty cow drinks water from, that body of water is as good as the Gangā, Yamunā, Sindhu or Sarasvatī. In the body of the cow, all holy places and rivers are present. The cow is the source of all nourishment and religious principles. Lakṣmī resides in cow dung. By offering respect to cows, one captures the four objectives of life (dharma, artha, kama and moksha). Therefore, all intelligent persons who desire benefit should offer obeisances to the cows."

Offering obeisances to the cow

namste jāyamānāyai jātāya uta te namaḥ
bālebhyaḥ śaphebhyo rūpāyadhnye te namaḥ

"O cow, who are not meant to be killed! I offer my obeisances to you, at the time of your birth and after your birth. I also offer obeisances unto your body, the hairs on your body, and to your hooves."

namo gobhyaḥ śrīmatībhyaḥ saurabheyibhya eva ca
namo brahmasūtābyaśca pavitrābhyo namo namaḥ

"I offer my obeisances to the cow, in whose body Lakṣmī resides. I offer my respects to the beautiful cow, for she is pure, simple, and aromatic. I bow down before the cow, who is the daughter of Brahmā.

She is pure internally and externally and she keeps the whole atmosphere pure by her presence. I repeatedly offer my obeisances unto her."

pañca gāvaḥ samutpannā
matthya māne mahodadhau
tāsāṁ madhye tu yā nandā
taśyai devyai namo namaḥ

sarvakāma dudhe devī
sarvatīrthā bhiṣecini
pāvani surabhi śreṣṭhe
devī tubhyaṁ namo namaḥ

"When the churning of the milk ocean took place, five cows appeared from it. Among them, the best one was known as Nandā. I offer my obeisances to her again and again. O best of the Surabhi cows, you fulfill all desires, and you are bathed by the waters of all the holy places. Therefore, O purifying agent, my repeated obeisances unto you."

yayā sarvamidaṁ vyāptaṁ jagat sthāvara
tāṁ dhenuṁ śirasā vande bhūta bhavyasya mātaraṁ

"I bow down to the cow, who pervades all animate and inanimate beings, and who is the mother of all who lived in the past, and who will live in future."

Serving the Cow

gaśca śuśruṣate yaśca samanvete ca sarvaśaḥ
tasmai tuṣṭāḥ prayacchanti varān api sudurlabhān
druhyonna manasā vāpi goṣu nityaṁ sukha pradaḥ
arcayet sadā caiva namaskāraiśca pūjayet
dāntaḥ prītamanā nityaṁ gavāṁ vyuṣtiṁ tathāśnute

"A person who serves the cow, and takes care of her in all respects, receives the most rare benediction from her. Do not become envious of the cow, even in your mind. Always try to please her and serve her as far as possible. Offer respect and worship her. A human being who joyfully serves the cow daily becomes fit to receive great prosperity."

The glories of the Cow From Mahābhārata,

In the *Ānuśāsana Parva, Dāna dharma Parva*, 51/26/34 The great sage Cyavana said to Nahuṣa, "O King, I do not see any wealth in this world equal to the cow. O protector of the subjects, hear and chant the glories of the cow, give cows in charity and see cows every day. The cow has been glorified in the *śāstras*. The cow is the source of prosperity. There is no tinge of sin in her. The cow always supplies food grains to the human beings, as well as the ingredients of sacrifice to the demigods. The cow is the mouth of sacrifice, she possesses divine nectar and releases it in the form of milk. The whole world bows down before her."

"In this world, the cow is equal to Agni, as far as her body and effulgence is concerned. She is the source of brightness and the giver of happiness to all living entities. Wherever cows live fearlessly, that place becomes sacred. The cow is the staircase to heaven. She is also worshiped in heaven. She fulfills all of one's desires. There is nothing superior to her."

"O best of the Bharata dynasty, I have thus revealed to you the glories of the cow. There are many more qualities that I have not mentioned. No one can completely describe all the good qualities of the cow."

Elsewhere in *Mahābhārata, Anuśāsana Parva, Dāna dharma Parva*, Chapter 69 Bhīṣma said to Yudhiṣṭhira, "O King, the cow, the land, and knowledge are very important objects. These things should be given in charity. The result achieved for donating these three things is the same. These three objects can fulfill all the desires of human beings. The cow is accepted as the mother of all living entities. She gives happiness to everyone. A person who wants advancement in material life should always live in the company of cows. One should always keep a cow. She is very auspicious. One should show respect for and worship the cow."

"The bull has been used for tilling the land since time immemorial. One should not unnecessarily give trouble to or disturb cows. If one mistreats a cow and does not take care of her properly then by her anger that person becomes destroyed. The temple and many other places are smeared with cow dung for purification. A person who daily feeds a cow even a morsel of grass certainly attains the result of observing many vows."

In the *Bhaviṣya-purāṇa, Uttara Parva*, Chapter 69 Lord Kṛṣṇa said to Yudhiṣṭhira, "O Pārtha, the five sacred cows which were produced during the churning of the Milk Ocean were Nandā, Subhadrā, Surabhi, Śusilā and Bahulā. They appeared just to benefit the people of the entire universe. The demigods then offered one of these cows to each of the great sages— Jamadagni, Bharadvāj, Vāsiṣṭha, Asita and Gautama. All these cows have the ability to fulfill all desires, thus they are known as Kāmadhenu."

"Milk, yogurt, ghee, cow dung, cow urine and *gorocanā*, which are produced from the cow, are very pure and they purify others also.

The sacred bilva tree, which is very dear to Śiva, and in which lives Lakṣmī, came into existence from cow dung. Later on, the seeds of blue and red lotuses were produced from cow dung. *Gorocanā*, which is produced from the cow's head, is very auspicious and it awards all perfection. The most fragrant *guggula* was produced from cow urine. Just the mere sight of cow urine makes one purified. This *guggula* is very dear to the demigods, and to Mahādeva in particular."

"All auspicious and palatable foodstuffs are prepared from cows' milk. Cow yogurt is required for the fulfillment of all kinds of desires. The nectar that is the favorite of the demigods is produced from ghee. A brāhmaṇa and ghee are not separate from each other. The *brāhmaṇas* possesses the Vedic mantras whereas the cow possesses the ingredients for sacrifice. A sacrifice is thus performed by the combined effort of the two. One's propensity for sacrifice comes from the cow. The cow is the abode of all the demigods. All the *Vedas*, as well as the literatures in pursuance of the *Vedas*, are present in the cow."

In the *Padma-purāṇa* , *Sṛṣṭi Khaṇḍa* 57/151-156 Lord Brahmā said to Nārada, "First, the *Vedas* appeared from the mouth of the Supreme Lord. Then gradually fire, the cow, and the *brāhmaṇas* appeared separately. In order to protect all the universes, I divided the one Veda into four, long ago. Agni and the *brāhmaṇas* accept the ingredients for worship on behalf of the demigods. The principle ingredients for sacrifice are produced from the cow. If these four objects had not existed, then the whole world would have been annihilated. Everyone, including the brāhmaṇas, demigods and demons should worship the cow because she is very liberal and the source of all good qualities."

"I created the cow long ago, for the nourishment of everyone. She is the form of the demigods and she is merciful to all living entities. Every object produced from the cow is pure. If one drinks pañcagavya, consisting of cow urine, cow dung, cow's milk, cow's yogurt and cow's ghee, all his sinful reactions become destroyed. That is why pious people daily use her products. The products of the cow are sacred and auspicious. A person who does not have the good fortune of consuming cow products is said to be unlucky, and his body is as good as stool."

"The influence of food grains remains in the body for five days, the influence of milk for seven days, the influence of yogurt for twenty-days and the influence of ghee for one month. For a person who does not eat cow products for one month- his food is shared by ghosts. Therefore, the cow has been accepted as the perfect item for all auspicious activities. The cow always awards the four objectives of life.

One who offers obeisances to the cow, and circumambulates her becomes liberated from all sinful reactions and enjoys heavenly pleasures. As Bṛhaspati, the spiritual master of the demigods, is worshipable, as Nārāyaṇa, the Lord of Lakṣmī is worshipable, so the cow is worshipable for all."

"The cow gives us milk and ghee. She is the source of ghee. May the cow which supplies us ghee and other products live in my house all the time. May the ghee always remain situated in my body and my mind. May the cow always remain in front of me, behind me, and by my side. May I always touch the cow and live next to her. In this way, one should offer prayers to her regularly and thereby become liberated from all sins. Lord Viṣṇu, the Ganga, and the *brāhmaṇas* are equally sacred. The cow is the form of religion, and the friend of the human beings. A house that does not have a cow is inauspicious."

In the *Agni-purāṇa* Lord Dhanvantari said to Ācārya Suśruta, "O Suśruta, the cow is pure and auspicious. All the planets are present in the body of the cow. Cow dung and cow urine vanquish all poverty. To caress and to bathe her is like cleansing ones sinful reactions."

"The six products of the cow are very auspicious, and they destroy the influence of a bad dream. Gorocanā can destroy the effect of poison, and it keeps the demons away. One who feeds a cow goes to heaven. A person, in whose house the cow lives pathetically, certainly goes to hell. If one feeds another's cow, he goes to heaven, and one who is active regarding cow welfare goes to Brahmaloka. The human beings, along with their family members, can be delivered by donating cows, by glorifying cows, and by protecting cows. The cow purifies the whole world by her presence. By touching the cow one exhausts his sinful reactions."

In the *Bṛhat Parāśara smṛti* it is written, "Simply by eating grass, the cows give us milk. From milk, ghee is produced, by which the demigods become satisfied, so how can one neglect the cow? Simply by her association a person becomes purified. By serving her, one achieves unlimited wealth, and by donating cows, one can transfer himself to heaven. There is no wealth superior to the cow. All the demigods live in the different parts of the cow's body. By serving the cow with devotion, Lord Hari becomes pleased. Her milk nourishes the human beings. How can such a cow not be worshipable?"

"By circumambulating the cow, one attains the result of circumambulating the whole world. One should give cows in charity and protect her in all respects. A foolish person who beats or chastises a cow goes to hell. A person who gives some food and water to a cow attains the result of performing the horse sacrifice- there is no doubt about it. A person who saves the life of even one cow, attains the result of giving one hundred cows in charity. How can a person suffer miseries if his house is adorned with cows? Rare are those who daily worship and serve the cow."

The glories of serving the cow are described in the *Viṣṇu-dharmottara-purāṇa* Part 3 , Chapter 291: Lord Haṁśa said, "O brāhmaṇas, by scratching the body of a cow and by removing the dust and worms from a cow's body one removes all his sinful reactions. One accumulates great piety by feeding a cow. By tending the cows in the field, one becomes eligible to live in heaven for countless years. By building a cowshed one becomes the king of the whole province. Simply by feeding her salt, one attains good fortune."

"O brāhmaṇas, if one delivers a cow from a dangerous situation or from the mud or from the fear of a tiger, one attains the result of performing a horse sacrifice. If one treats a sick cow with medicine, one can become cured of his own sickness. Simply by making her fearless, one also become fearless. If one saves a cow from the hands of a *caṇḍāla*, one attains the result of performing the cow sacrifice. By protecting a cow from heat and cold, one goes to heaven. You should treat the cow with great respect."

"O brāhmaṇas, maintain your livelihood with the products received from cows. This is called *go-vṛta.* For one who does this for one full month, all his sinful reactions are destroyed. Giving a cow in charity to a brāhmaṇa destroys all of one's inauspiciousness. One who does so goes to Brahmaloka in an airplane as bright as the sun."

"O brāhmaṇas, the dust from cows' hooves purifies all sins. It does not matter if that dust is from a holy place or from a contaminated place, like Magadha or Kīkata. There is no doubt about it. The cow is all-auspicious, purifying and the giver of prosperity. The place where the cow lives is purified. It is very auspicious to touch a cow because this destroys one's bad dreams and sinful reactions."

"The Ganges personally lives in the head of the cow. Any place smeared with cow dung is considered pure. That is why the sacrificial arena and the cooking place are first smeared with cow dung. Lakṣmī lives in cow dung, Gangā lives in cow's urine, Soma lives in cow's milk, yogurt and ghee, and Sarasvatī lives in Gorocanā. The ancient *ācāryas* have accepted the cow as the form of Lord Viṣṇu. The cow is fit to be worshiped, glorified and offered obeisances. A human being should feed the cows and serve her."

"O brāhmaṇas, by serving the cows people become purified and free from distress and lamentation."

Nothing is Rare for a Devotee of the cow,

(From *Mahābhārata*, *Anuśāsana Parva* , 83/50 to 52)

goṣu bhaktaśca labhate
yad yadiccati mānavaḥ
strio' pi bhaktā yā goṣu
tāsca kāma mavāpnuyuḥ

putrārthi labhate putram
kanyārthi tāmavāpnuyāt
dhanārthi labhate vittam
dharnārthi dharmamapnuyāt

vidyārthi cāpnuvāt vidhyam
sukhārthi prāpnuyāt sukham
na kiñcid durlabham caiva
gavāṁ bhartasya bhārata.

"O Bhārata, nothing is rare for a devotee of the cow. Whatever such devotees desire, they achieve. A lady who is devoted to the cow can have her desires fulfilled, by the cows' mercy. One who desires a son, one who desires a daughter, one who desires wealth, one who desires piety, one who desires knowledge- all can get their desires fulfilled by the mercy of the cow."

The Contribution of the Cow in the Pastimes of Lord Rāmacandra

According to the *Vedas*, there are seven mothers. The cow is one of them. These mothers are- one's own mother, the wife of the spiritual master, the wife of a brāhmaṇa, the queen, the cow, the nurse, and the earth. The cow is considered the mother of the universe. When Lord Brahmā desired to undertake the work of creation, he first created the cows among all living entities.

In the *Mahābhārata*, *Anuśāsana parva*, Chapter 145 it is stated:

lokān sisṛkṣuṇā pūrvaṁ
gāvaḥ sṛṣṭāḥ svayaṁbhuvā
vṛtyarthaṁ sarvabhūtānāṁ
tasmāt tā mātaraḥ smṛtāḥ

"Mother cow is the personification of the motherly energy. The day when there will be no cows left in this world, it will be bereft of a mother and thus no other living entities will survive. The cow is the opulence of the material world. The sages survive on the cows, and various religious activities are performed by the support of the cows."

Sage Vaśiṣṭha has said in the *Vālmiki Rāmāyana*:

śāśvatī śabalā mahyaṁ
kīrtir ātmavato yathā
asyāṁ havyaṁ ca kavyaṁ
prāṇa yātrā tathaiva ca

āyattam agnihotraṁ ca
balir homas tathaiva ca
svāhā kāra vaṣaṭ kārau
vidhyāśca vividhāś tathā

"As the pious deeds of an intelligent person are never separated from him, the cow that awards happiness cannot be separated from me. My performance of sacrifices and my livelihood are dependent on the cow. My knowledge regarding the Vedic literatures is under the shelter of the cow."

In these statements the unique usefulness of the cow is described. Indeed, if one carefully studies the pastimes of Śrī Rāma, one can find that the cows had a special role to play in them. When the Supreme Lord descends into this world, He needs support. Śrī Rāma is no exception. The pastimes of Śrī Rāma are divided into five categories. Childhood pastimes, Marriage pastimes, Forest pastimes, Battle pastimes and King pastimes. In all of these pastimes, cows had a role to play.

The cow was the indirect cause of Lord Rāmacandra's appearance. When the inhabitants of the material world were disturbed by the demons, Lord Brahmā, along with the cow, prayed to the Supreme Lord. Being pleased by their prayers, Lord Hari appeared as the son of Daśaratha and Kauśalyā.

Daśaratha performed a sacrifice in which he donated ten lakh cows. This sacrifice was meant to invoke the appearance of Lord Rāmacandra. Under the order of Vaśiṣṭha Muni, the great sage Śṛngī conducted the sacrifice. In that sacrifice, Agni came with a golden container, having some divine sweetrice in it, and he gave it to King Daśaratha and told him to feed it to his queens. After eating the sweetrice, the queens became pregnant and in due course of time, Śrī Rāma, along with His brothers, appeared. The mother of Rāma used to donate cow ghee, so that the child Rāma would not be affected by evil spirits.

Yogurt was a favorite food of Lord Rāmacandra. Even before his marriage, Śrī Rāma was asked to give a cow in charity. He gave away four lakhs cows. The horns of these cows were covered with gold. He also donated to the *brāhmaṇas* the same number of brass pots, for milking the cows.

When Śrī Rāma was about to go into exile in the forest, everyone was filled with lamentation. At that time, Rāma asked Lakṣmana to satisfy the sages Agastya and Viśvāmitra by giving them one thousand cows each. He also donated one thousand cows to Citraratha. He arranged to give twelve hundred bulls to those brahmacārīs who were engaged in studying the scriptures, so that they could use them to carry their food grains. He also gave them one thousand cows, so that they could eat the products of those cows.

There is a nice incident in Rāmāyana in this regard. Rāma was ready to go to the forest. At that time, the wife of a poor and weak brāhmaṇa named Trijaṭa asked her husband, "O Lord, please go and meet Rāmacandra and you will certainly get something from Him. He is very religious minded."

Trijaṭa went before Rāmacandra and said, "I am very poor and I have many children. Please be kind to me."

On hearing these words, Śrī Rāma replied, "O great brāhmaṇa, throw your stick as far as you can and all the cows that are situated within the area the stick passes over will belong to you."

Trijaṭa tightened his dhoti and threw his stick with great force. This stick flew in the sky and fell to the ground on the other side of the river Sarayu. As agreed, Śrī Rāma gave him all of those cows in charity. The brāhmaṇa became very happy and returned home.

To protect the cows and the brāhmaṇas, Śrī Rāma killed the witch Tāḍaka. One reason for the battle between Rāma and Rāvana was the cow. Rāvana was always inimical to the cows. He ordered his followers to burn those countries where *brāhmaṇas* and cows live.

When Rāmacandra returned to Ayodhyā after killing Rāvana, He was greeted, among others, by the cows that had accompanied the Lord. During Rāma's coronation ceremony, He donated one lakh horses, one lakh milk cows and one hundred bulls. It is stated in the Rāmāyana that Rāmacandra had performed innumerable horse sacrifices in which He donated innumerable cows. During His rule, the cow was highly respected, and it was the duty of everyone to serve the cow. Rāma and Sītā used to regularly worship Kāmadhenu, and feed her cooked food.

More on the Contribution of the Cow in the Pastimes of Lord Kṛṣṇa:

The abode of Kṛṣṇa is Goloka. He appeared in this world and set the ideal example of how to serve the cows. This is why He is addressed as Govinda, Gopālanandana, and so on. Another name of Kṛṣṇa is Gopāla, the maintainer of cows. When Kṛṣṇa was born, Nanda Mahārāja gave thousands of cows to the brāhmaṇas. The cows were very dear to all of the residents of Braja, and Kṛṣṇa in particular.

In Their childhood, Kṛṣṇa and Balarāma used to play with the calves. They pulled their tails and chased them all over the place. The residents of Braja, and especially the gopīs, took great pleasure in watching Kṛṣṇa play with the calves.

When He was a little grown up, Kṛṣṇa used to go to the pasturing ground, to tend the cows. The main profession of the Brajavāsīs was to trade milk products. Kṛṣṇa's pastimes with the cows are described in *Śrīmad-Bhāgavatam* , Gopāla-campū, Ānanda-vṛndāvana-campū and many other literatures.

In *Śrīmad-Bhāgavatam* 10/8/24 it is stated as follows: "Within the house of Nanda Mahārāja, the cowherd ladies would enjoy seeing the pastimes of the babies Rāma and Kṛṣṇa. The babies would catch the ends of the calves' tails, and the calves would drag Them here and there. When the ladies saw these pastimes, they certainly stopped their household activities and laughed and enjoyed the incidents."

In *Gopāla-campū*, the following statements are found: "My dear friend, just see how Kṛṣṇa and Balarāma are playing. They are surrounded by some other friends. They are all laughing and enjoying their pastimes. See how Kṛṣṇa and Balarāma have caught hold of the calves' tails. They have really become very naughty. They know how to trouble everyone. Did you see how They were quarreling with their mother the other day? There is no doubt that They are very expert in the art of quarreling."

Elsewhere in *Śrīmad-Bhāgavatam* , 10/44/15 it is stated as follows : "The ladies of Vraja are the most fortunate of women because, with their minds fully attached to Kṛṣṇa and their throats always choked up with tears, they constantly sing about Him while milking the cows, winnowing grain, churning butter, gathering cow dung for fuel, riding on swings, taking care of their crying babies, sprinkling the ground with water, cleaning their houses, and so on. By their exalted Kṛṣṇa consciousness they automatically acquire all desirable things."

In the *Gopāla-campū*, these following statements are found: "O Yaśodā, your son is repeatedly doing mischief. You know what He has done today. He comes to our Goshalā and unties the cows. We think that He does this by your approval. Otherwise, how does He dare do such mischievous things? If you say that He does not do so by your approval, then why don't you chastise Him?

In the *Gopāla-campū*, the following passage is also found: "Kṛṣṇa and Balarāma have really become restless. Their favorite sport is with the cows. If They cannot live without the cows then let them go to the forest with the calves to tend them."

Sage Vasiṣṭha's Service to the Cow

Our religious scriptures, histories and *Purāṇas* are filled with glorification of the great sage, Vasiṣṭha. His wife, Arundhatī, is a chaste and ideal lady. She resides by her husband's side and serves him faithfully. Realizing that Śrī Rāmacandra will appear in this world, Vasiṣṭha, who is the son of Lord Brahmā, accepted the post of family priest for the Surya dynasty. He considered himself fortunate to have Śrī Rāma as his disciple. He was always engaged in the welfare of all living entities. Whenever there was drought or famine, he made it rain, and he protected the living entities from immature death by the power of his austerities. By his instructions, Bhagiratha brought the Ganges to this world.

Sage Vasiṣṭha was a great ascetic, and the personification of forgiveness. When Viśvāmitra killed his one hundred sons, he did not react or curse him, even though he had the power to do so. This shows his forgiveness and detachment. His whole life was absorbed in love for Śrī Rāma. He instructed Rāma in various ways. Even today, he is living among the seven sages and continuing his welfare activities for all.

It is well known how much Vasiṣṭha is devoted to the cow. With the help of his cow, Śabala, he treated the great sage Viśvāmitra and his followers to a royal reception. This is described in the Rāmāyana. He used to serve the cows with his own hands. Indeed, both he and his wife used to regularly worship the cow, because he knew very well the importance of serving the cow. That is the reason why he would always stay at a place where there are cows. He gave instructions to King

Saudāsa about service to the cows. This is described in *Mahābhārata* as follows:

gāvaḥ surabhi gandhinyas
tathā guggulu gandhayaḥ
gāvaḥ pratiṣṭhā bhūtānām
gāvaḥ svastyanaṁ mahat

The great sage, Vaśiṣṭha, said "O King, many varieties of aroma emanate from the body of the cow. As such, many cows are as fragrant as guggula resin. The cow is the support of all living entities, and an ocean of auspiciousness."

gāvo bhūtaṁ ca bhavyaṁ ca
gāvaḥ puṣṭiḥ sanātanī

gāvo lakṣmās tathā mūlaṁ
goṣu dattaṁ na naśyati

"The cow is the past and future. She nourishes the health of all living entities and she is the root of prosperity. The piety one achieves by feeding a cow is never destroyed."

nā kīrtayitvā gāha supyāt
tāsāṁ saṁsmṛtya cotpatet
sāyāṁ prātar namasye ca
gāstataḥ puṣtimāpnuyāt

"Do not go to bed at night without praising the cow. Do not get up in the morning without remembering the cow. Offer respect to the cow daily, every morning. By doing so, a human being achieves strength and nourishment."

gāśca saṅkīrtaye nityaṁ
nāva manyeta tāstathā
aniṣṭaṁ svapramālakṣya
gāṁ naraḥ samprakīrtayet

"Chant the name of the cow daily and never insult her. If one sees a bad dream, one should immediately remember the cow."

gāvai paśyāṁyahaṁ nityaṁ
gāvaḥ paśyantu māṁ sadā
gāvo' smākaṁ vayaṁ tāsāṁ
yato gāvastato vayaṁ

"May I always see the cow and may the cow always see me. The cow belongs to me and I belong to the cow. I wish to always live in a place where there are cows."

In this way, Vasiṣṭha has imparted us nice instructions about service to the cows. He concluded that if human beings sincerely take care of the cow, they will attain all kinds of benefit. He had celebrated cows, like Śabalā and Nandini. By serving Nandini, King Dilip and his wife, Śudakṣina, gave birth to King Raghu. He instructed all learned persons, as well as all neophyte Sanskrit students, to serve the cows.

Once upon a time, the *kṣatriya* king, Viśvāmitra, arrived with his army at the āśrama of Vasiṣṭha. He had more than one hundred thousand soldiers with him. The sage had his cow, named Śabalā. Actually, it was her who prepared delicious food for all these guests. Viśvāmitra and his army became very satisfied, but at the same time, he was struck with wonder and began to think about how the sage had arranged such a huge quantity of delicious food. When he came to know about Śabalā, he asked Vasiṣṭha if he could have that cow.

Indeed, he agreed to pay the sage a huge amount in exchange. But the sage did not agree.

At this point, King Viśvāmitra ordered his army to take away Śabalā by force. Thereafter, when the soldiers began to drag her, she cried and asked the sage, "Why are you giving me away?"

The sage replied, "I am not giving you away. This king is very powerful. He does not listen to my words and wants to take you forcibly."

Just then, Śabalā produced from her body innumerable *yavanas*, *khasas*, *pahallavas*, and huṇas, who killed all the soldiers of Viśvāmitra in a short time. This incident is described very nicely in the *Rāmāyana*, 1/54/18 to 23.

It is difficult to estimate how much devotion Vasiṣṭha has for cows, and how powerful mother cow can be. Therefore, all human beings should serve the cows with great respect. She awards benefit to everyone equally.

The Great Sage Cyavana's Devotion to the Cow

Once, the great sage Cyavana gave up pride, anger, and lamentation and took a firm vow to perform austerities for twelve years under water. Soon he became friendly to the aquatics.

One day, some fishermen spread their net in the water of the Ganges. When they pulled their net out of the waster, they captured many aquatics, along with the sage, Cyavana. The fishermen became afraid upon seeing the sage. They fell at the feet of the sage and begged pardon. Because of being pulled out of the water, the aquatics began to die. Upon seeing their pathetic condition, the sage became very compassionate.

In reply to the fishermen's questions the sage then said, "If these fish live, then I will also live, and if they die, then I will die with them. I cannot leave them."

After hearing these words, the fishermen became fearful. They immediately went to their king, Nahuṣa, and told him about the incident. The King, along with his ministers and priest, quickly went to see the sage.

The King folded his hands and introduced himself to the sage. He then asked, "O best of brāhmaṇas, please order me, how can I serve you?"

The sage replied, "These fishermen have worked hard today. Pay them the price of me and all of these fish."

The King immediately ordered his priest to give one thousand gold coins to the fishermen. But, the sage interrupted the King and said, "One thousand gold coins is not my actual price. Think properly and then pay them the reasonable price."

In this way, King Nahuṣa raised the price of the sage from one thousand gold coins, to one million gold coins, and then to ten million gold coins and finally, to half of his kingdom. Still, the sage did not agree. He said, "I don't consider my worth to be half of your Kingdom. Please discuss this with the sages and then decide on a correct price."

Upon hearing the sage's words, the King became perplexed and so he began to consult his ministers and priests. At that moment, another sage, who lives on fruits, and who was born from the womb of a cow, came there and said, "O King, I know how to satisfy this sage."

The King asked him to reveal the actual price of Cyavana, thus saving his kingdom and dynasty. The sage replied, "Just as *brāhmaṇas* are topmost among all members of the varṇas, and as such no one can estimate their worth, similarly, no one can estimate the price of a cow. Therefore, you should give one cow in exchange for this sage."

The King then informed Cyavana of this verdict and requested him to be merciful. The sage said, "O King, now I am pleased, for you have rightly fixed my price. Actually, in the whole world there is no wealth superior to a cow."

Thereafter, by the mercy of the sage, the fishermen and the aquatics became purified and went to heaven. The King also became very happy and from that time onward, he began to worship the cows. The great sage then returned to his hermitage.

King Ṛtambhara's Service to the Cow

There was a King named Ṛtambhara. He had many wives, but he had no children. One day, the sage Jāvāli came to his palace. After greeting and serving him nicely, the King asked him how he could receive a son. The sage said that by the mercy of Lord Viṣṇu, the cow, or Lord Śiva, one can get a son.

When the King further asked him about how to serve and worship the cow, the sage replied, "O King, one who wishes to serve cows should personally take them to the field for tending. If one wants a son, he should feed barley to his cows. Then, when the barley comes out with the dung, he should collect it, wash it and then eat it. He should feed the cow first, and then he himself should eat. He should make sure that the cows are not disturbed by mosquitoes and other insects. If you personally do all of these things, mother cow will certainly give you a pious son."

According to these instructions of the sage, the pious King began to serve his cows with great devotion. One day, as the King was tending the cows, he became captivated by the natural beauty of the forest and began to relish it. At this time, a lion suddenly came from another forest and killed one of his cows. The cow had lowed loudly in fear, so that the King immediately came running. When he saw that one of his cows had been killed by a lion, the King became extremely unhappy.

He kept his composure, however, and approached Sage Jāvāli, informing him about the entire incident. He then inquired from the sage about how he could become relieved from this sin, as well as how he could receive a son.

The sage replied, "There are different kinds of atonement prescribed in the scriptures to destroy one's sinful reactions. If you follow such atonement with proper rules and regulations, you can become purified. However, if one knowingly kills a cow or blasphemes Lord Nārāyaṇa, he can never be delivered. A fallen person who even thinks of giving trouble to a cow, lives in hell for a duration of time equal to the rule of fourteen Indras. An unfortunate person that purposely criticizes the Supreme Lord and troubles the cow certainly suffers in hell. But, there is a procedure for being relieved of the sin of killing a cow unknowingly. You should go to King Ṛtuparṇa, for he can give you proper advice."

Being thus ordered, the King went to see Ṛtuparṇa, who was very pious and a devotee of Śrī Rāma. After being informed of everything that the sage had advised, the pious, powerful and intelligent

King said with a smile, "The sage, Javali, is a great personality whereas I am very insignificant. Why did you leave him and came to me? If you have faith in me then kindly hear my words."

"O noble King, sincerely worship, with your body, mind and speech, Śrī Rāma, who is the Lord of the universe. If He becomes pleased by your worship, He will fulfill all of your desires, and destroy the sin you have incurred by allowing one of your cows to be killed."

Soon, by the advice of Ṛtuparṇa, King Ṛrambhara became purified by worshiping Śrī Rāma. He dedicated his life for the welfare of all living entities, especially the cows. Being pleased by his service, the merciful Kāmadhenu appeared before the King and awarded him his desired benediction. After doing so, she suddenly disappeared. As a result of her benediction, King Ṛtambhara got a pious and devoted son, named Satyavāna.

Satyakāma's Achievement of Spiritual Knowledge by Service to the Cow

There was a pious *brāhmaṇa* lady named Jabālā. She had a son named Satyakāma. When he grew up and became mature enough to study, he said, "O mother, I want to go and live at the gurukula. When my master asks me about my name and lineage, what should I say?"

His mother replied, "My dear son, I did not get an opportunity to ask your father about his lineage, because in those days, I was extremely busy taking care of guests. So, when your master asks you, simply say that you are Satyakāma, the son of Jabālā."

Satyakāma approached his master, the sage Gautama, and said, "I wish to stay here and serve you as a bramacārī."

The master inquired, "My dear son, what is your lineage?"

Satyakāma replied, "O Lord, I do not know what is my lineage. But my name is Satyakāma Jāvālā."

Sage Gautama said "My son, no one other than a *brāhmaṇa* can speak so frankly. Go and collect some wood for sacrifice, I will give you initiation."

After initiation, the sage gave him four hundred cows and some ox to take care of. He instructed that when the number of cows reached one thousand, he should return. Satyakāma went to the forest with the cows and built a cottage there. He began to look after the cows with great devotion.

After some time, when there were one thousand cows, a bull came before Satyakāma and said, "My dear son, now you should take us to the *āśrama* of our master. Let me give you an instruction regarding spiritual truth. It is this: 'brahman is light'. You will receive more instructions from Agni."

Thereafter, Satyakāma departed for the *āśrama* of his master. It was far, so he had to halt at some place. Then, he arranged for the cows to drink water and take rest. After doing so, he lit a fire and sat down. The personification of fire then said to him, "Let me give you another instruction regarding spiritual truth. It is this: 'Brahman is unlimited'. The next instruction you will receive from Haṁśa."

The next evening, Satyakāma had to again halt at some place, while proceeding to his master's *āśrama*. As he and the cows were about to take rest, a swan came flying through the sky, speaking to Satyakāma. He said, "O Satyakāma, let me tell you the third instruction about spiritual truth. It is this: 'Brahman is effulgent.' The forth instruction you will receive from a water bird."

The next evening, Satyakāma halted under a banyan tree. As he sat down, after lighting a fire, a water bird came before him and said, "My dear son, let me tell you the fourth instruction regarding Brahman. It is this: 'Brahman is vast'."

In this way, he received knowledge from various sources about the supreme truth. Thereafter, Satyakāma, along with one thousand cows, arrived at the hermitage of his master. When his master saw him, he said, "O Satyakāma, you look very bright. It appears to me that you have realized the Supersoul."

Satyakāma replied, "My lord, I have received knowledge from living entities other than human beings."

Thereafter, the sage Gautama instructed Satyakāma fully about spiritual truth with great pleasure.

King Dilīp's Love for the Cow

King Dilīp and Indra were good friends. Once, Indra invited the King to come with him to heaven. Later, while coming from heaven, the King saw a Kāmadhenu in the sky, but he was so eager to return home that he did not pay much attention to her. Indeed, he did not even offer his obeisances to Kāmadhenu. As a result, Kāmadhenu became angry and cursed the King, saying, "If my son does not show mercy to you, you will remain childless."

King Dilīp did not even hear the curse. But later on, it so happened, that he, along with his queen and subjects, became unhappy because of his having no son. With a desire to attain a son, he and his wife went to the āśrama of his family priest, the sage Vasiṣṭha. After hearing their request the sage said, "Stay in my āśrama for some time, and serve my cow, Nandini."

The King obeyed the order of his spiritual master. His queen Sudakṣiṇā would regularly worship the cows, early in the morning. The King would then personally take Nandini to the forest for grazing. After spending the whole day with the cow in the forest, the King would return to the āśrama of his master. The queen would then greet the cow and circumambulate her. In this way, both the king and the queen used to take care of the cow with great devotion.

After twenty-one days had passed in this way, while tending Nandini, the King lost his concentration for a moment. Suddenly, he heard a scream and saw Nandini had been attacked by a lion. The King was so shocked that he could not take up his bow and arrow to kill the lion. He simply stood there and breathed heavily with anger.

At that moment, the lion spoke to the King, in the voice of a human being, "O King, your weapon is useless, just like a storm, although capable of uprooting a tree, becomes ineffective while assaulting a mountain. My name is Kumbhodara. I am the friend of Lord Śiva's associate, Nikumbha. Lord Śiva made me a lion and ordered me to protect this forest from the attack of the wild animals, such as elephants. Whoever comes in the path of my vision becomes my prey. This cow had entered my forest without permission. Besides this, she had come at a time when I am hungry. Therefore, I will eat her and mitigate my hunger. Do not feel embarrassed and unhappy. Simply return home."

But King Dilīp, who was very kindhearted, felt great distress upon seeing the pathetic condition of Nandini, and thinking about her calf.

The motherly affection of Nandini appeared more important to the King than his own life and so he prayed to the lion to eat him in exchange for the cow. The lion ridiculed this proposal, saying, "O King, you are the proprietor of the entire earth. You can satisfy your spiritual master by giving him millions of milk cows. Why are you about to give your life in exchange for this insignificant creature? I think that you have lost your good sense."

"If you have really taken a vow to do good to others and if I eat you today in exchange for the cow, then you will have only saved one life. But, if you remain alive, you will be able to save many lives in the future. Therefore, save your own body, which is the source of your happiness. To give voluntary distress to your body, for the purpose of attaining heaven, is totally useless for rich people like you. Heaven? It is present in this world only. A person who has all arrangements for sense gratification is supposed to be living in heaven. Only weak and distressed people desire to go to heaven."

After hearing these words of the lion, who was a servant of Lord Śiva, the most merciful King Dilīp looked at the pathetic Nandini, who was begging for her life. The King, upholding his kṣatriya spirit, said, "No, lion, I cannot go back after having allowed you to eat her flesh. I do not wish to pollute the kṣatriya community. We are famous in this world for protecting others from danger. Enjoying the kingdom is not our aim in life. Therefore, you can eat my flesh and leave this cow alone. After all, this body is temporary and will be finished some day. For this reason, it is not proper for people like me to become attached to the body."

Thereafter, the King threw away his weapons and went before the lion, to be eaten by him. Just then, the Vidyādharas began to shower flowers on the King, from the sky. Nandini then said to the King, "My dear son, please get up."

The King became surprised to see Nandini, while not being able to see the lion anywhere. Nandini said, "O Pious King, to test you, I created this lion. By the influence of Vasiṣṭha, even Yamarāja cannot give me trouble, and so what to speak of other living entities. I am very pleased by your devotion to your spiritual master, and by the compassion you have shown me. Now, you can ask me for a benediction. Do not think I am an ordinary cow. I am Kāmadhenu, who fulfills everyone's desires."

The King folded his hands and begged her to give him a son who would continue his dynasty. Nandini agreed, and asked the King to milk her and drink the milk. Nandini became very happy by the patience of the King. They both returned to the āśrama of their master. In due course of time, the King was benedicted with a powerful son, named Raghu, and his devotion to the cow became an ideal example for others to follow.

King Virāṭa's Treasury of Cows

The cow makes a great contribution towards the prosperity of a country. Not only for the householders, but also for the sages and ascetics, the cow is very important. There are many instances in the scriptures of kings that gave away many cows in charity to the sages and *brāhmaṇas*. One such instance is found in *Mahābharata*.

King Virāṭa ruled the country known as Matsya deśa. He was very famous for having many cows in his kingdom. His rival kings were envious of him because of this. The five Pāṇḍava brothers, along with Draupadi, lived incognito within Virāṭa's kingdom. Once, Duryodhana sent spies to find out where the Pāṇḍavas were living. His spies came to Virāṭa's kingdom, and were surprised to see the huge number of cows there.

Duryodhana then made a plan to steal these cows. He thought that if the Pāṇḍavas were hiding there, they would certainly come out of hiding to protect Virata's cows. On the other hand, if they were not at that place, he would still not be the loser, because he would gain so many cows. Therefore, he invaded Matsya deśa and stole all of Virata's cows. However, it came to be that by the help of the Pāṇḍavas, the King recovered all of his lost cows.

Sahadeva, the youngest among the Pāṇḍava brothers, when he visited Virāṭa's kingdom, he talked with the king about the subject of cows. From their conversation, as related in the *Mahābhārata*, it is clearly understood that the kings in those days used to take care of innumerable cows and make all necessary arrangements for their protection. It is stated that King Virāṭa's cowshed was right next to his palace.

Sahadeva had introduced himself as having formerly looked after the cows of Maharaja Yudhisthira. His job had been to count the cows and look after them. He informed the King about the Pāṇḍavas' huge number of cows, their various categories, the method of counting, and the arrangements made for their service. According to him, King Yudhiṣṭhira had eight lakhs cows. He had many quarters, each housing one hundred cows. He described how he had looked after one lakh of a certain variety of cow, and two lakhs of yet another. In this way, Sahadeva said that he had been the director of the Pāṇḍavas' cows. Because of this, he was called 'Tantipāla'.

Sahadeva had a special power by which he could tell about the past, present and future of any cow that was situated within an area of ten yojanas. King Yudhiṣṭhira knew very well of Sahadeva's unique abilities. Thus, he was very pleased with him. Sahadeva also knew how to quickly increase the number of cows, and how to keep the cows from becoming ill. He also knew the symptoms of good quality bulls. Sahadeva even knew which bull, simply by the smell of it's urine, a childless woman would become eligible for pregnancy.

From these statements it appears that in those days, cow protection was very developed and all of the big kings had nice arrangements for keeping cows. King Virāṭa had one hundred thousand cows.

Some of them were of one colour and some were multi-coloured. All of these cows were adorned with various qualities. The King had many cowherd men to take care of his cows. These men were not only expert in the art of looking after cows, but were also expert in the art of fighting. When Trigarta, the friend of the Kauravas, attacked and tried to steal King Virāṭa's cows, these cowherd men strongly fought with him. Finally, Arjuna defeated the Kaurava army in a fierce battle, and freed all of the stolen cows. Only after this did the Pāṇḍavas' exile come to an end. From this incident, one can just imagine how important it is to serve and protect cows.

The Story of Surabhī

Once, in reply to the question of Nārada, Lord Nārāyaṇa said that the original mother of all cows is Surabhī, who lives in Goloka. She is the source of all cows. It was Surabhī who first appeared in Vṛndāvana, from Goloka. Once, Śrī Rādhā-Kṛṣṇa, in the company of many gopīs, went to the forest of Vṛndāvana. They sat down in a solitary place. Kṛṣṇa then suddenly developed a desire to drink milk. Immediately, out of His own sweet will, He manifested the Surabhi cow from His left side. Her milk bag was filled with milk. The name of her calf was 'Manoratha'. Sudāmā, who was present there, immediately took a new pot and began to milk her.

This milk was just like nectar and was capable of destroying the occurrence of birth and death. Kṛṣṇa, who is the Lord of the gopīs, personally drank that milk. Suddenly, the milk pot fell out of His hands and broke. All the milk spread on the ground, and took the shape of a lake. This lake was one hundred yojanas wide and one hundred yojanas long.

This lake is famous in Goloka as Kṣīra-sarovara. It has become the principal spot for Śrī Rādhā and the other gopīs to enjoy their pastimes. All four sides of this lake were plastered with various jewels. By the will of Kṛṣṇa, immediately, innumerable Kāmadhenus appeared there. The same number of gopīs also appeared from the pores of these cows. These cows had countless calves. This is how, by the mercy of Surabhī, all of the cows were created and came to fill the entire universe.

At that time, Lord Kṛṣṇa personally worshiped the Surabhī cow. From that time onward, worship of the cow continued in this world.

On the next day, (Dīpāvalī), the worship of Surabhī took place by the order of Kṛṣṇa.

The Lord said, "O fortunate soul, one should worship and meditate upon the Surabhī cow. The six syllable mantra for worshiping Surabhī is 'oṁ Surabhai namaḥ'. If a person chants this mantra one hundred thousand times, he attains perfection and all of his desires become fulfilled. I also worship the goddess Surabhī, who is the giver of enjoyment, intelligence, and liberation, and who is the form of Lakṣmī, the companion of Rādhā, the predominating deity of the cows, and the most purifying object. One should worship Surabhī by thinking her to be present within a pitcher, the head of a cow, in the post used for tying the cow, in a Śālagrāma-śīla, in water and in fire. The cow should be particularly worshiped on the day of Dīpāvalī. One who worships the cow- he himself becomes worshipable in this world."

Once, during the Vārāha kalpa, the goddess Surabhī stopped giving milk. As a result, the three worlds experienced a scarcity of milk. All of the demigods became worried and so they went to Brahmaloka and began offering prayers. Indra, the leader of the demigods, offered prayers to Surabhī in this way: "O devī, I offer my obeisances unto you. O mother of the universe, you are the original cause of the cows. My obeisances unto you."

"O you, who are very dear to Śrī Rādhā. My repeated obeisances to you. You are very dear to Śrī Kṛṣṇa . You created all of the cows. My obeisances to Surabhī, who is like the desire tree, and who is always ready to give all kinds of benediction. You are also known as Śubhā, Śubhadrā and Gopradhā. My repeated obeisances unto you, for you are the giver of fame, piety, and good deeds."

As soon as mother Surabhī heard this prayer, she became pleased and appeared before the demigods in Brahmaloka. The goddess gave Indra a rare benediction and then returned to her abode, Goloka. The demigods also returned to their respective abodes. Suddenly, the entire universe became filled with milk. Ghee was made from the milk and then used in sacrifice. Anyone who faithfully hears this purifying prayer will attain the wealth of cows, prosperity, fame and good children. He will also attain the result of bathing in all the holy places. Such a person will go back to Godhead at the end of his present life.

The Story of the Appearance of Godāvarī

This story took place at the time when the great sage, Gautama, used to live in the Brahmagiri hills. There was once a terrible famine due to severe drought. There was a great scarcity of food grains all over the country. At that time, sage Vasiṣṭha, along with some other sages, went to Gautama's āśrama. Gautama greeted them properly and then fed them with nice food grains. Every morning, the sage, Gautama, would sow seeds in the field, and by the power of his austerity, they would mature by evening. These food grains would then be collected and used for feeding the sages.

It finally rained again after twelve years. Because of this, the hot surface of the earth became cooled. Indeed, all directions came to look green. At that time, the most chaste Parvatī said to her husband, Lord Śiva, at Kailasa mountain, "O Lord, you keep the Ganges on your head, but you keep me on your lap. In this way, you insult me."

However, Lord Śiva did not pay any attention to her words. Because of this, Pārvatī became somewhat angry. She then went to her son Ganeśa and told him about this. Ganeśa felt unhappy, upon seeing his mother's distress. Then he, along with his elder brother, Kārtikeya, went to the *āśrama* of sage Gautama, in the guise of *brāhmaṇas*.

They said, "O sages, the famine has come to an end. The entire earth has again become filled with grains and water. Now, you do not need to stay in this āśrama any longer."

These words of Ganeśa and Kārtikeya had an impact on the minds of the sages. They immediately began preparing to leave. Sage Gautama then said, "I have protected your lives by supplying food during the time of famine. Now, you should not leave me in this way, without my permission. I request you to stay here some more time."

On hearing these words of Gautama, the sages gave up their plan to leave. Ganeśa then said to Kārtikeya, "You assume the form of a cow and stand in Gautama's field. When the sage sees you, fall down to the ground and pretend like you are dead."

Kārtikeya did exactly as he was told. When the other sages saw this, they once again decided to leave. Then, when Gautama again requested them to stay, they replied, "This place has become inauspicious, due to the death of a cow. If, however, you can bring the Ganges here like Bhagīratha did, and also bring the cow back to life, we will reconsider our decision."

After hearing this, the sage Gautama went to Trambaka mountain and performed austerities, to summon the Ganges. Finally, Lord Śiva became pleased by his *tapasya* and agreed to send the Ganges to his *āśrama*. Sage Gautama requested, "My Lord, may the Ganges deliver the cow and then merge her into the water of the ocean? In this way, kindly make me glorious."

Lord Śiva replied, "So be it. The Ganges will now become famous as Gautamī and Godāvrī."

After speaking in this way, Lord Śiva put the Ganges in the hands of Gautama, who then returned to his āśrama at Brahmagiri. In this place, the Ganges is divided into three streams. One stream went toward the south and merged into the ocean. Another stream pierced the coverings of the universe and went to Pātālaloka. And the third stream went to heaven through the sky. The Ganges that went towards the south is known as Gautamī or Godāvarī.

The Importance of Service to the Cow is Described in Śrīmad-Bhāgavatam

Although Vedic literatures have awarded the cow an exalted position, at present, respect for cow has come down so much that everywhere, cows are seen to be in a very miserable condition. There is a lack of internal faith and devotion for the cow. People should follow the example set by Lord Kṛṣṇa Himself, in regard to the service of the cow.

In the *Śrīmad-Bhāgavatam* it is stated (7/4/16) that during the time of Hiraṇyakaśipu, the whole world was very prosperous. All necessities of life were supplied in abundance and yet he was still not satisfied because his senses were uncontrolled. He used to trouble and cause anxiety to the devotees, sages, human beings and demigods. When the demigods prayed to the Lord for relief, they were assured by the following verse (7/4/27).

yadā deveṣu vedeṣu
goṣu vipreṣu sādhuṣu
dharme mayi ca vidveṣaḥ
sa vā āśu vinaśyati

"When one is envious of the demigods (who represent the Supreme Personality of Godhead), of the *Vedas* (which give all kinds of knowledge), of the cows, the brāhmaṇas, the vaiṣṇavas, and religious principles, and ultimately of Me, the Supreme Personality of Godhead, he and his civilization will be vanquished without delay."

This is the eternal arrangement of providence. There is no difference between mother earth and mother cow. Whenever mother earth feels the burden of miscreants, she assumes the form of a cow and narrates her distress to the Supreme Lord.

Once, King Parikṣit was traveling in his kingdom, when suddenly he saw a bull with only one leg, and a very miserable cow. She was shedding tears, as if her calf has died. The King soon understood the cause for this, and so he assured the cow with the following words. (SB 1/17/9 & 10)

mā saurabheyātra śuco
vyetu te vṛṣalād bhayam
mā rodīr amba bhadraṁ te
khalānāṁ mayi śāstari

yasya rāṣṭre prajāḥ sarvās
trasyante sādhvy asādhubhiḥ

tasya mattasya naśyanti
kīrtir āyur bhago gatiḥ

"O son of Surabhi, you need lament no longer. There is no need for you to fear this low class śūdra. O mother cow, as long as I am living as the ruler of this Earth, and the subduer of all envious men, there is no cause for you to cry. All will be well for you."

"O chaste one, the king's good name, duration of life and good rebirth vanish when all kinds of living beings are terrified by miscreants in his kingdom."

The cow is very dear to the Supreme Lord. This was confirmed by the Lord Himself, when he spoke the following verse to the sages headed by Sanaka.
(SB 3/16/10)

ye me tanūr dvija-varān duhatīr madīyā
bhūtāny alabdha-śaraṇāni ca bheda-buddhyā
drakṣyanty agha-kṣata-dṛśo hy ahi-manyavas tān
gṛdhrā ruṣā mama kuṣanty adhidaṇḍa-netuḥ

"The brāhmaṇas, the cows and defenseless creatures are My own body. Those whose faculty of judgment has been impaired by their own sin look upon these as distinct from Me. They are just like furious serpents, and they are angrily torn apart by the bills of the vulture-like messengers of Yamarāja, the superintendent of sinful persons."

Those who discriminate against certain classes of beings, and who thus do not treat all living entities equally, are severely punished. When Pṛṣadhra, the son of Manu, accidentally killed a cow while protecting it from a hunter, he had to suffer the curse of his spiritual master. Thereafter, he had to undergo severe austerities, to become purified. There was no leniency shown to any person who gave trouble to the cow in previous ages.

The glories of the cow are described throughout *Śrīmad-Bhāgavatam* . In the tenth canto of *Śrīmad-Bhāgavatam* , chapter one, text eighteen, it is stated that when the earth was tormented by sinful kings, she took the form of a cow and prayed to the Supreme Lord for relief, along with the demigods, headed by Brahmā.

Lord Śiva's Devotion to the Cow

(From *Skanda-purāṇa, Nāgara*, Chapter 258-259)

Once, Lord Śiva committed some offense against sages who possessed divine power. The sages cursed him gravely. Being afraid of the curse, Lord Śiva went to Goloka and began to offer prayers to Surabhi, who is considered to be a form of the brāhmaṇas.

He said, "O Mother, you are the cause of creation, maintenance and annihilation. My repeated obeisances unto you. Through your affectionate nature, you satisfy human beings, demigods and the forefathers. You are the giver of nectar to all. This is the verdict of all great personalities. You have distributed strength and affection to all moving and non-moving living entities."

"O Goddess, you are the mother of the Rudras, the daughter of the Vasus and the sister of the Ādityas. You award the desired result to those who satisfy you. You are Dhi, Tuṣti, Svāhā, Svadhā, Ṛddhi, Siddhi, Lakṣmī, Kīrti, Mati, Kanti, Lajjā, Mahāmāyā and Śraddhā. You award the objectives of life. There is nothing within the three worlds other than you. You please Agni and the demigods. You pervade the entire universe."

"O Goddess, you are the benefactor of all living entities, and you are the abode of all the demigods. Therefore, please do something about my body."

"O sinless one, I humbly adore you. Kindly be pleased with me. O Source of nectar, my body is burning by the fire of the brāhmaṇas' curse. Please relieve me of this calamity."

After praying in this way, Lord Śiva circumambulated Surabhī and then entered her body. Mother Surabhī then kept Lord Siva within her womb. Meanwhile, not seeing Lord Śiva anywhere, the demigods became full of anxiety. They then satisfied those *brāhmaṇas* and came to know that Lord Śiva had gone to Goloka. The demigods also went to Goloka, where the mud is sweet rice, the rivers are filled with ghee, and the lakes are filled with honey. The inhabitants of that planet walk around with yogurt and nectar in their hands.

In Goloka they saw the effulgent son of Surabhī called Nīla. It was Lord Śiva who appeared from Surabhī in the form of a bull called Nīlavṛṣabha. The demigods also saw varieties of cows in Goloka. They are known as Nadā, Sumanasā, Svarūpā, Śiśīlakā, Kāminī, Nandinī, Medhyā, Hiraṇyadā, Dhanadā, Dharmadā, Narmadā, Sakalapriyā, Vāmanalambikā, Kṛṣṇā, Dīrghaśṛṇgā, Supicchikā,Tārā, Toyikā, Śāntā, Dūrvisahyā, Manoramā, Sunāsā, Gaurā, Gaurmukhī, Haridrāvarṇā, Nīlā, Ṣaṇkhinī, Pañcavarṇikā, Vinatā, Abhinatā, Bhinnavarṇā, Supatrikā, Jayā, Aruṇā, Kuṇḍoghnī Sudatī and Cārucampakā. They saw Nīlavṛṣabha playing happily with them. His body was red, his mouth and tail were yellow and his hooves and horns were white.

This Nīlavṛṣabha was none other than Mahādeva. He was the four pillars of religious principles and he was the five-headed Mahādeva. Simply by his darśan one attains the result of performing the vājpeya sacrifice. By worshiping Nīla, one automatically worships the whole universe. By feeding the bull green grass one satisfies the entire universe. In the body of Nīla lives Lord Janārdana. The demigods pleased Nīla by offering many prayers.

They said, "O Lord, anyone who behaves with you rudely certainly becomes a fit candidate for hellish conditions. One who touches you with his feet suffers the miseries of hunger and thirst, and one who becomes cruel towards you can never attain liberation. Being glorified by the demigods in this way, Nīla offered his obeisances to those demigods and sages. The demigods also gave him the boon that he would be released among the cows and be marked with a trident and a disc so that he would benefit the whole world.

Why is Lord Śiva called Vṛṣabhadhvaja and Paśupati ?

(*Mahābhārata Anuśāsana parva*, Chapter 77)

One day, the calf of Surabhi was drinking her milk. While drinking, a drop of foam suddenly fell on the head of Mahādeva, who was sitting nearby. When Lord Śiva became very angry at this, Prajāpati said to him, "O lord, a drop of nectar has fallen on your head. The milk of the cow never becomes contaminated because of drinking by the calf. As the moon showers nectar, similarly cows shower nectar. As nectar drunk by Vāyu, Agni, and the other demigods does not become contaminated, in the same way, the cow does not become contaminated while feeding milk to her calf. These cows will nourish the whole universe with their milk and ghee. Everyone will aspire to relish their nectarean milk."

After speaking in this way, Prajāpati gave a few cows to Mahādeva. Lord Śiva then happily made the bull his carrier and he decorated his flag with the mark of a bull. This is how he became known as Vṛṣabhadhaja. Then, the demigods awarded Lord Śiva the name Paśupati, the Lord of the animals. The cows are the most important and beneficial objects in the entire world. Lord Śiva always lives with the cows. She is soothing, peaceful, and pure, and she is the sustainer of all living entities.

Topics About the Cow in Ancient History:

Sāyaṇācārya explained the *Ṛg-veda*. He wrote in his commentary that in the beginning of the creation, there were human beings and cows. At first, none of them spoke. Finally a cow opened her mouth and then human beings also began to speak. Therefore, human beings received the power of speaking from cows.

There are three different descriptions regarding the appearance of the cow:

1. Lord Brahmā was drinking nectar through one of his mouths. Then from another mouth came foam, from which appeared Surabhī.

2. Prajāpati Dakṣa was the progenitor of human beings. He had sixty daughters. One of them was Surabhī.

3. In order to benefit the entire universe, the demons and the demigods once churned the ocean. In the course of this churning, 14 jewels were produced. Surabhī is one of them. From Surabhī came the Kapilā cow. From her milk, the ocean of milk was created. In the beginning, the color of the cow was golden, but by the angry glance of Lord Śiva, they received different colors.

It is said that one day, Lord Śiva went to see Brahmā. The grandfather greeted him with due respect and gave him so many cows in charity that it appeared as if the opulence of heaven was insignificant. Lord Śiva became very happy and since then, he has become renowned as Paśupati. At this time, Lord Śiva also accepted the bull called Nandi as his carrier.

Bāṇāsura was the king of Śoṇitpur (Present day Nepal). He was a great devotee of Lord Śiva. One day, being pleased with Bāṇāsura, Lord Śiva donated twelve cows to him. With the help of these cows, the king became very powerful and influential.

The king had a beautiful daughter named Uṣā, who fell in love with Kṛṣṇa's grandson, Aniruddha. When the King came to know about this, he arrested Aniruddha. Meanwhile Nārada informed Lord Kṛṣṇa of this, and so He took His huge army and went to Śoṇitpur. When Bāṇāsura heard the news, he called his ministers for consultation. He did not mind losing his kingdom, but he never wanted to lose his cows.

Finally, he decided to keep his cows with Kubera, on the condition that he should not give them to anyone without his permission. Bānā lost the battle and then entered into an agreement with Kṛṣṇa.

When Kṛṣṇa was about to leave for Dvārkā, along with Aniruddha and Uṣā, someone whispered in His ear, "O Lord, You forgot one thing. Bāṇāsura has twelve unique cows that he has kept hidden with Kubera."

For this reason, Kṛṣṇa changed His plan. Kubera was then told to return the cows, but he did not agree. As a result, war was declared against Kubera and so the demigods became frightened. Many peacemakers tried to pacify both parties. Finally they convinced Kṛṣṇa to forget about the cows, and in this way, war was avoided.

Rāvana, the king of the demons, used to regularly circumambulate the cows. Ikṣvāku's grandson fought in a battle, while riding on the back of a kakud or bull. That is why the dynasty of Lord Rāmacandra is also known as Kākutstha.

Once upon a time, King Kārtavirya Arjuna, along with his huge army, went to the āśrama of the great sage Jamadagni. The sage greeted the king and served him nicely with the help of his cow, Kāmadhenu. However, the king became attracted to the cow and so asked the sage to give it to him. The sage refused to give him the cow, and so the king took it away by force. When the sage tried to stop him, the king chopped of his head.

At this, the sage's wife, Renukā, began to scream. At that time, the famous son of Jamadagni, named Paraśurām, was engaged in meditation at a nearby mountain. When he heard his mother's cry, his meditation broke. He came home quickly and became extremely angry when he saw his father's condition. Thereafter, for a number of years, he fought and killed numerous kṣatriyas. In fact, he killed all the kṣatriyas of the world twenty-one times.

It is said that the great sage, Dattātreya, used to wander about with his cow, dog and deer. King Janaka donated one thousand cows to his priest, the sage Yājñavalkya.

There is an interesting story regarding the birth of Gaṇeśa. As soon as Gaṇeśa was born, Māhadeva cut off his head by mistake and the head disappeared. Because of this, Parvati cried terribly. The physicians of the demigods, the Aśvini Kumars, were summoned and somehow replaced the head. In exchange for this service, they asked that they be given Mahādeva as their fee. This caused a complex problem. All the demigods had a discussion about this and finally they gave one cow to the Aśvini Kumars, in exchange for Mahādeva. Because of this, Parvati felt greatly relieved. The physicians were also very happy.

A nice incident took place in the life of Lord Buddha. Once, he fasted for forty-nine days but still, he could neither attain knowledge nor liberation. He then renounced all worldly connection and traveled to many places in search of liberation. One day, he was sitting under a banyan tree near Gayā.

A beautiful girl named Sujāta, who lived near that place, pledged to the predominating deity of the banyan tree that if her desire were fulfilled, she would offer sweet rice made with the milk of sixteen hundred cows. Her desire was fulfilled and so she took sixteen hundred cows to a nearby field for tending. She then milked these cows and fed the milk to eight hundred cows. The next day, she milked those eight hundred cows and fed the milk to four hundred cows. Then again, she milked the four hundred cows and fed it to two hundred cows.

In this way, she finally milked eight cows and prepared nice sweet rice. She placed the sweet rice on a golden plate and went to the banyan tree. As she approached, she saw the personified banyan tree sitting there, and so Sujāta became very happy. Gautam Buddha accepted her sweet rice, and immediately he attained knowledge and realized the path of liberation, for which He had been in anxiety for a long time.

King Nṛga gave one hundred thousand cows in charity to the brahmanas. When Bharat met Rāmacandra, Rāmacandra asked him, "O brother, do the cowherd people love you? Is cow protection going on nicely?"

In this way, in previous ages, there was a great respect for the cow. This principle should be followed at all times.

The Universal Form of the Cow

(from *Atharva-veda* 9/7/1 to 26):

"All the demigods live in the body of the cow. Prajāpati and Parameṣṭhi are her horns. Indra is her head, Agni is her forehead and Yamarāja is her throat. The king of all the stars (the Moon) is her brain, Dyuloka is her upper jaw, and the Earth is her lower jaw. Lightning is her tongue, the Maruts are her teeth, the star Revati is her throat, the star Kṛttikā is her shoulder and the summer season is her shoulder bone. Vāyu is her bodily limbs, her residence is heaven and Rudra is her back bone."

"The Hawk is her chest, the sky is her strength, Bṛhaspatī is her hump and the chanda known as Bṛhati is her chest bones. The celestial women are her back and the maidservants of those women are her ribcage. Mitra and Varuṇa are her shoulders, Tvaṣṭā and Aryamā are her hands, and Mahādeva is her arms. The wife of Indra is her back portion, Vāyu is her tail and Pavamāna is her bodily hair. *Brāhmaṇas* and Kṣatriyas are her milk bag, and Bala is her thighs. Brahmā and the Sun god are her two knees, Gandharvas are her calf muscle, Apsaras are her small bones, and Aditi (the mother of the demigods) is her hoof."

"The mind is her heart, intelligence is her stomach, and vows are her veins. Hunger is her belly, Saraswati is her intestine and mountains are her internal portions. Anger is her kidney, lamentation is her uterus, and the subjects are her reproductive parts. The river is her womb, the rainy season is her milk-bag, and clouds are her nipples. The universal energy is her skin, herbs are her bodily hair, and the stars are her beauty. The demigods are her private parts, human beings are her intestines and yakṣas are her belly. The demons are her blood and other living entities are her stomach. The sky is her fat and death is her bone marrow."

"When the cow is sitting, she is the form of Agni. When she is standing, she is the form of the Aśvini Kumāras. When she is standing, facing east, she is Indra, and when she is standing, facing south, she is Yamarāja. When she is standing, facing west, she is the form of Brahmā, and when she is facing north, she is the form of the Sungod. When she is eating grass, she is the form of moon, and when she looks, she is the demigod Mitra. When she turns, she is happiness. When she in the form of a bull, pulling a cart or plough, she is Viśvadeva. When she is ploughing, she is Prajāpati, and when she is let loose, she is everything. This is the universal form of the cow. One who understands this form of the cow properly possesses many different kinds of domestic animals.

The *Bṛhat Parāśara-smṛti,* 5/34 to 41 states: "Lord Brahmā lives at the root of the cow's horns and Lord Nārāyaṇa lives in the middle of the horn. On the top of the horn lives Lord Śiva. In this way these three personalities live in the horns of the cow. In the front portion of her horn all holy places are situated. Indeed, all of the demigods live in the body of the cow."

"Goddess Pārvatī lives on her forehead, Kārtikeya lives in her nose and in her two ears live two Nāgas named Kambala and Aśvatara. In the right eye of that surabhī cow lives the Sungod, and in her left eye lives the Moongod. In her teeth live the eight Vasus, and in her tongue lives the demigod Varuṇa. Goddess Sarasvatī lives in the sound of lowing, and Yama and Yakṣa live in her two cheeks. The sages live in the pores of her body, and the pure water of the Ganges is the form of her urine. Yamunā resides in the cow dung."

"Two hundred eighty million demigods live in the pores of her skin. Agnī lives in her stomach and Dakṣin Agnī lives in her heart. The Āhavanīya Agnī lives in her mouth and in her ribs live Sabhya Agnī and Āvasathya Agnī. In this way, one who understands that all of the demigods reside in the body of the cow, and thus does not display any anger at her, can attain great opulence and heavenly residence."

The *Padma Purāna, Sṛiṣṭi Khaṇḍa* 57/ 156 to 165) states: The entire Vedic literatures live within the mouth of the cow. On her horns live Lord Viṣṇu and Śankara. Kārtikeya lives in her belly, Brahmā in her head, Mahādeva in her forhead, Indra on the tip of her horn, Aśvini Kumāras live in her two ears, the sun and the moon live in her two eyes, and Garuḍa lives in her teeth. Goddess Sarasvatī lives in her tongue, all holy rivers live in her anus, the Ganges lives in her vagina, the sages live in the pores of her skin, and Yamarāja lives on her face."

"Varuṇa and Kubera live on the right side of her back, Yakṣa and Tejasvi live on the left side of her back, the Gandharva lives inside her mouth, and the Nāgas live in the tip of her nose. The Apsarās live in the back portion of her hooves. Lakṣmī lives in the cow dung, Pārvartī lives in her urine, the demigods who wander in the sky live in the front portion of her legs, Prajāpati lives in her sound of lowing, and the four oceans live in her milk bag."

"A person who daily touches the cow after taking his bath becomes liberated from all sinful reactions. One who smears himself with the dust from the hooves of the cow is said to have taken bath in all holy places. Such a person becomes freed from all types of sin."

The *Bhaviśya-Purāṇa, Uttara Parva*, 61/ 25 to 37) states: "Lord Brahmā and Lord Viṣṇu live in the root of the cows horns, all the holy places are present in the tip of her horns , Mahādeva lives in the middles of her horns, Gauri resides in her forehead, Kārtikeya resides in the tip of her nose, and the two Nāgas Kambala and Aśvatara live in her two nostrils. The Aśvinī Kumāras live in her two ears, the sun and the moon live in her eyes, the eight Vaśus live in her teeth, Varuṇa in her tongue, Sarasvati in her throat, Yama and Yakṣa in her two cheeks, morning and evening are present in her two lips, Indra in her shoulder, the demons in her hump, the sky lives in her heels, and Dharma lives in her four legs."

"Gandharvas live in the middle of her hoof, the snakes live in the front portion of the hoof and the demons live in the back portion of her hoof. The eleven Rudras live on the back of the cow, Varuṇa in all the joints, the forefathers in the waist, the human beings in the cheek, and Śrī is situated in her anus. The rays of the sun are situated in her hair, Gangā is situated in her urine, and Yamunā is situated in cow dung."

"Three Hundred and thirty three million demigods live in the pores of her bodily hair. The mountain and the earth are situated in her belly, in her four nipples live the four oceans. The demigod Parjanya lives in her milk, and the clouds live in the drops of her milk. The gārhapatyāgni lives in her stomach, dakṣināgni lives in her heart, āhavaniyāgni lives in her throat, and sabhyāgni lives in her palate. The mountains live in her bones, and sacrifices live in the bone marrow. The four *Vedas* are also situated within the body of the cow."

The *Brahmāṇḍa-purāṇa* states: "O Lord of the universe, Nārāyaṇa! I offer my respectful obeisances unto you. Long ago, Shrila Vyāsadeva spoke about the Gosāvitrī stotra. Now I will describe it. This prayer to the cows destroys all sinful reactions and awards one his desired goal. Thus, it is very auspicious. Vedavyāsa Himself, who is an incarnation of Lord Viṣṇu, lives in the tip of the cow's horns. Parvatī lives in the root of her horns, Sadāśiva in the middles of the horns, Brahmā in her head, Bṛhaspati in her shoulder, Śankara in her forehead, the Aśvinī Kumāras in her ears, the Sun and the Moon in her eyes, the sages in her teeth, Sarasvatī in her tongue and all of the demigods in her chest."

"The Gandharvas live in the middle of her hoof, the Moon and Ananta live in the front portion of her hoof, and the Apśaras live in the back of her hoof. The forefathers live in her back, the three material qualities live in her eye-brows, the sages live in her pores, Prajāpati lives in her skin, the Sky lives in her chin, Yamarāja lives in her back, all the holy places are situated in her anus, and Gangā is present in her urine. Lakṣmī resides in her vision, her back and the dung. The Aśvinī Kumārās live in her two nostrils and Caṇḍikāka lives in her lips. The four oceans reside in her milk bag, Sāvitri and Prajāpatikā are present in the sound of her lowing. Indeed, the cow is also directly the form of Lord Viṣṇu. Lord Keśava is present in her entire body."

The *Skānda-purāṇa. Āvantya Khaṇḍa* , *Revā Khaṇḍa*, Chapter 83 states: "All demigods live in the body of the cow, and all the *Vedas* are present in cow dung. Indra lives in the tip of her horns, Kārtikeya in her heart, Brahmā in her head, Śankara in her forehead, the Sun and the Moon in her eyes, Sarasvatī in her tongue, the Maruts in her teeth, the four *Vedas* in the sound of lowing, the sages in the pores of her body, Yamarāja on her back, and the oceans on her milk bag."

"Her urine has emanated from the lotus feet of Lord Viṣṇu and simply by seeing it, one can destroy his sinful reactions. Lakṣmī lives in cow dung, the Gandharvas, Apsaras and Nāgas live in the tip of her hooves. Apart from this, all the holy places and rivers are also present within the body of the cow. Lord Viṣṇu is the source of all the demigods, and the cow is born from the body of Lord Viṣṇu.

That is why human beings consider the cow to be inclusive of all the demigods."

The *Mahābhārata, Aśvamedhika Parva, Vaiṣṇava-dharmaParva* Chapter - 92 states: Lord Kṛṣṇa said to Maharaja Yudhiṣṭhira, " O King, when a brown cow is given to a brāhmaṇa in charity, at that time, Lord Viṣṇu and Indra live on the tip of her horns. Indra and the Moon reside in the root of the horn, Brahmā lives in the middle of the horn, Śankara lives in her forehead, the Aśvinī Kumāras live in the ears, the sun and the moon live in her eyes, the Maruts live in her teeth, Sarasvtī lives in her tongue, the sages in her pores, Prajāpati in her skin, and all Vedic literatures live in her breath."

"The aroma of fragrant flowers lives in her nostrils. The Vasus live in her lips and Agni lives in her mouth. The Sādhya demigods live in her rib cage. Pārvatī lives in her throat, the stars live on her back, the sky lives in her hump, all holy places live in her anus, Gangā is directly present in her urine, and Lakṣmī is situated in her dung. The most beautiful goddess, Jyeṣṭhā, lives in her nose, the forefathers live in her milk bag and goddess Ramā lives in her tail. The Viśvadevas live on both sides of her ribs. Kārtikeya lives in her chest, and the five kinds of bodily air live in her knees and thighs. The Gandharvas live in the middle of her hooves, the Nāgas live in the front side of her hooves, and the four oceans live in her four nipples."

In conclusion, the author lists the ten faults in regard to eating meat:

1. Meat eating is detrimental to achieving of the Supreme Lord.
2. Meat eating displeases the Supreme Lord.
3. Meat eating is a grave sin.
4. Meat eating causes distress in this life and in the next.
5. Meat eating is against the nature of human beings.
6. Meat eating causes one to achieve animal propensities.
7. Meat eating is a human being's illegal endeavor.
8. Meat eating is grave cruelty.
9. Meat eating destroys one's health.
10. Meat eating is condemned in the *śāstras*.